21世纪商务英语系列教材

新编外贸英语教程

主　编　任素贞
副主编　张其云　王　灏
参　编　高媛媛　于巧峰
　　　　姚明海　徐　飞

图书在版编目(CIP)数据

新编外贸英语教程/任素贞主编.—北京：北京大学出版社,2012.8
(21世纪商务英语系列教材)
ISBN 978-7-301-16271-2

Ⅰ.①新… Ⅱ.①任… Ⅲ.①外贸—英语—教材 Ⅳ.①H319.9

中国版本图书馆 CIP 数据核字(2012)第 257425 号

书　　　名：	新编外贸英语教程
著作责任者：	任素贞　主编
责 任 编 辑：	李　颖
标 准 书 号：	ISBN 978-7-301-16271-2/H・3119
出 版 发 行：	北京大学出版社
地　　　址：	北京市海淀区成府路 205 号　100871
网　　　址：	http://www.pup.cn
电　　　话：	邮购部 62752015　发行部 62750672　编辑部 62754382　出版部 62754962
电 子 信 箱：	zbing@pup.pku.edu.cn
印　刷　者：	北京虎彩文化传播有限公司
经　销　者：	新华书店
	787 毫米×1092 毫米　16 开本　10.25 印张　254 千字
	2012 年 8 月第 1 版　2021 年 8 月第 4 次印刷
定　　　价：	38.00 元

未经许可，不得以任何方式复制或抄袭本书之部分或全部内容。
版权所有，侵权必究
举报电话：(010)62752024　　电子信箱：fd@pup.pku.edu.cn

前　言

国际化进程不断加速，国际贸易日益频繁，如何把握机遇并成功进行国际化交流、交际和交易离不开智慧和策略的载体——信函。成功的信函会吸引新客户、稳定老客户、招徕潜在客户。为此，青岛科技大学外国语学院几位富有深厚专业知识积淀和丰富教学经验积累的教师为您精心编写了这部商务函电教材。

本教材编写团队为商务英语函电优秀课程组的教师，他们不仅具有国外访学的国际视野、丰富的一线教学经验，而且具有外贸实战经历；另外，所培养的众多从事经贸行业的毕业生也成为他们强大的资源信息后盾。

在筛选不同行业多家贸易公司和货代公司的邮件、合同、代理协议以及单据的基础上，编者们确保教材内容的全面系统，既传承经典，又紧跟时代步伐。

本教材以实用性为目标、以规范性为出发点、以全面性和系统性为指导原则、以精益求精为服务宗旨、以广大学生和国际商务工作者为读者目标，真诚奉献该团队多年辛勤积累的成果。

教材共有11章，以信函格式、建立业务关系、报盘还盘、成交签约、执行合同、包装、运输、保险、索赔、理赔等流程为主线。每一部分穿插国际贸易背景知识与理论知识导入，提供不同形式和内容的信函样本，增添具有鲜明时代特色的辅助阅读材料，标注适当的专业术语及生词注释，并且针对每一章内容设计形式多样的练习题。

通过各个部分的学习，读者能够系统掌握国际货物买卖的一般程序、惯例和规则，了解国际贸易实务流程各个业务环节及与之有关的银行、保险、运输等服务运作层面的英语专业术语、常用句式，把握信函的篇章构成和主要单证文书的语言表述特点等。读者可在原有英语读写能力的基础上融会贯通、灵活应用有关业务知识和语言技能，极大提高阅读、撰写、翻译对外贸易有关书信的能力，熟练掌握国际商务往来中不同类型信函写作模式和交际策略的同时，进一步提高使用英语进行跨文化交流、交际和交易的能力。

尽管我们力求严谨零差错，然而百密难免会有一疏，倘有任何差错，敬请广大读者不吝赐教！

编　者

2012.8

Contents

Chapter One	Layout and Principles of Business Letters	1
Chapter Two	Channels of Establishing Business Relations	10
Chapter Three	Enquiries and Replies	20
Chapter Four	Offers and Counteroffers	31
Chapter Five	Conclusion of Business	42
Chapter Six	Payment	63
Chapter Seven	Establishment of and Amendment to L/C	76
Chapter Eight	Shipment	89
Chapter Nine	Insurance	106
Chapter Ten	Complaints and Claims	121
Chapter Eleven	Résumé, Memorandum, Notes and Fax	137
Appendix		147
参考文献		158

Chapter One

Layout and Principles of Business Letters

Part I Introduction

Business letters are traditionally written in a formal and set style for commercial purpose, usually used when one business organization writes to another, or for correspondence between such organizations and their customers or clients and other external parties. The overall style of such a letter depends on the relationship between the parties concerned. Nowadays, business letter-writing tends to be less formal and more friendly, yet it still follows a certain layout.

A business letter usually consists of 10 parts:

- Letter-head/sender's address: name, postal address, phone, fax number and email address of the sender;
- Date: the formal date can be written as Oct. 25, 2012 in the American style (British style: 25th Oct., 2012), while the informal one can be written as 25/10/2012;
- Reference number;
- Inside address/recipient's address: the name and complete address of the correspondent or organization to which the letter is sent;
- Salutation: the popular ones are Dear Sir or Madam, Dear Sirs, or Ladies and Gentlemen;
- Subject line/Attention line;
- Body of the letter;
- Complimentary close such as: yours faithfully/yours truly, etc.;
- Signature and position;
- Enclosures.

Some parts, such as reference number, attention line and enclosures, might be omitted for the sake of convenience.

Part II Sample Letters

Sample 1

James & Sons Ltd.
67 Madison Square, Melbourne B.C. 3
Australia

31st Dec., 2011
Our ref.: 376
Your ref.:W.P.T.2

24 Jilong Rd.
China Machinery Imp. & Exp. Corp.
Guangzhou
P. R. C.

Gentlemen:

<u>100 Cases Walnut Meat</u>

Further to our letter of 15th Dec., in which we informed you that the above consignment has been stopped by the Medical Officer of Health, we enclose a copy of the relevant "Stop Notice" and a report issued by Messrs Oliver Clark & Co. Ltd., London, independent Surveyors and Assessors.

These documents will support the information given in our previous letter and, in addition, we are forwarding, under separate cover, a jar containing sample of the contaminated walnut meats sealed by the Wharfingers.

The goods are at present in process of being screened and fumigated and we shall in due course be rendering a Debit Note for the cost.

Looking forward to your reply.

Yours truly,
Encl.

Sample 2

Ken's Cheese House
34 Chatley Avenue Seattle, WA 98765

Oct. 23, 2011

Fred Flintstone

Sales Manager
Cheese Specialists Inc.
456 Rubble Road
Rockville, IL

Dear Mr. Flintstone:
With reference to our telephone conversation today, I am writing to confirm your order for 120 cases of Cheddar Cheese Ref. No. 856. The order will be shipped within three days via UPS and should arrive at your store in about 10 days.
Please contact us again if we can help in any way.

Yours sincerely,
Kenneth Beare
Director of Ken's Cheese House

Sample 3

China Textiles Import & Export Corporation
35 Chongming Rd., Xiaojiao, Beijing
P. R. C.

20th Nov., 2010
Ref. No.: GB33

Lanka Textiles Co.
P. O. Box 665
Colombo
Sri Lanka

Dear Sirs,

In response to your letter of 15th, enquiring for bed-sheets, we wish to inform you that the sample-cutting book, price list and catalogue required have been airmailed to you separately. We are confident that these will provide you with all the details you require. However, if you are in need of any other information not contained therein, please feel free to let us know. We shall satisfy you to the best of our ability.

Your payment terms by L/C at sight are acceptable to us. In order to ensure the punctual shipment of the goods to be ordered, please see that the covering L/C reaches us at least 30 days before the stipulated timed of shipment.

We look forward to your orders soon.

Yours faithfully,

Quiz:

(1) There are three styles of layout above: the blocked form which means all the typing lines start from the left-hand margin; the indented form which means the traditional style; the third style is a kind of blending between the blocked and the indented. Now please tell: _____ letter is in blocked form; _____ is in indented form and _____ is a blending form.

(2) A business letter is usually composed of _____（信头）, _____（案号及日期）, _____（封内名称和地址）, _____（称呼）, _____（事由）, _____（信文）, _____（结尾敬语）, _____（签名）and _____（附件）. Now can you find out these different parts in the above letters? Do you think the inside name and address stands for the writer or the receiver? Or both?

(3) Is there any mistake in the Complementary Close of the third letter? If yes, how to correct it?

(4) Where's the position of the Subject Line? Above or below the Salutation?

(5) Do you write the word "No." before the number of an address or not? For instance, how do you translate the address 松岭路99号 into English?

Part III Business Email Writing

With the popularity of the Internet, more and more people use email to communicate for its quickness and convenience. The following are some tips to help you for writing business letters through email.

- A heading is not necessary in an email (your return address, their address, and the date).
- Use a descriptive subject line.
- Avoid using an inappropriate or silly email address; register a professional sounding address if you don't have one.
- Use simple formatting, keep everything beginning with the left margin; avoid special formatting and tabs.
- Keep your letter formal. Even if it is an email instead of a hard copy, there is no excuse for informality (Don't forget to use spell check and proper grammar).
- Try to keep your letter less than 80 characters wide. Some email readers will create line breaks on anything longer and ruin the formatting.
- If possible, avoid attachments unless the recipient has requested or is expecting an attachment. If it is a text document, simply cut and paste the text below your letter and strip out any special formatting.
- If the person's name is unknown, address the person's title, e.g. Dear Director of Human Resources.

Chapter One

Part IV Sample Emails

Sample 1

To: HK supplier
Subject: Walkie Talkie

Dear Madam/Sir,

We are a UK importer of many products and we are looking for promotional items for Christmas. Please can you provide the following information on your products? Volume would be in the region of 10,000 units.

Please provide an image of the products, packaging, your best price, dead time, international standards met.

We look forward to your early reply.

Yours sincerely,
Mr. John Citizen

UK Buyer

Sample 2

Business Email Sample

To: "Anna Jones" <annajones@buzzle.com>
Cc: All Staff
From: "James Brown"
Subject: Welcome to our Hive!

Dear Anna,

Welcome to our Hive!

It is a pleasure to welcome you to the team of _____. We are excited to have you join our team, and we hope that you will enjoy working with our company.

On the last Saturday of each month we hold a special staff party to welcome any new employees. Please be sure to come next week to meet all of our senior staff and any other new staff members who have joined _____ this month. You will receive an e-mail regarding the same with further details.

If you have any questions during your training period, please do not hesitate to contact me. You can reach me at my email address or on my office line at 000-0001.

Warm regards,
James

Jackie Brown, Manager, Staff
jamesbrown@abcd.com
Tel: 000-0001

Part V Envelope

Although people do not use envelopes to send letters as they used to, it is still essential for us to know how to write an envelope in a correct way. Below is an example.

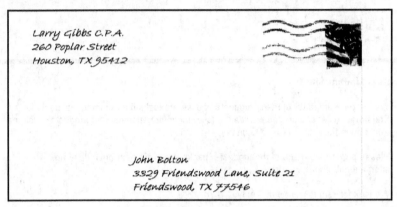

Part VI Principles of Successful Communication

1. List the points to be communicated

You are expected to list all the points you are going to converse and arrange them in a logical order. If you are replying to a letter, then underline those parts which require reply or comments. In this way, you can not only ensure your writing is complete but also avoid wordiness or repetition. Paragraphing carefully can make your writing clearer and easier to read, while confining each point or topic to one paragraph can help your readers to focus on your topics.

2. Keep the balance between clarity and conciseness

Clarity and conciseness should go hand in hand. You are not supposed to achieve conciseness at the risk of clarity since it matters what you want to tell or to achieve clarity at the cost of conciseness in view of the fact that time is precious. To achieve such purpose, write briefly and completely so that the readers can better understand what you are driving at.

3. Be courteous and considerate

Being courteous and considerate means treating the reader with respect, friendliness, sincerity on the one hand and being tactful, thoughtful and appreciative on the other hand. It requires you to employ good human relation skills, which are of great importance in establishing business credit. So remember to reply letters promptly. Conflicts and discrepancies are inevitable. They should be tackled with sincerity and tactics.

4. Put yourself in the reader's shoes

Try to imagine you are the reader and how you would feel about what you write. Try to be persuasive, apologetic, sympathetic, firm, complaining and so on. The right tone will help to arouse the good will, warmth, cooperation and interest in your reader to ensure the possibility of achieving your purpose.

5. Check your letters

Be careful to create a good impression with each of your letter. Before sending it out, check it for the accuracy of its contents, and test its general suitability against such questions as the following:
- Is its appearance attractive or well laid out?
- Is there any spelling mistake or grammatical mistake?
- Does it cover all the essential points and is the information given correct?
- Is what I have written clear, concise and courteous?
- Does it sound natural and sincere?
- Does it adapt to the reader's point of view and will it be readily understood?
- Is its general tone right and is it likely to create the impression intended?
- Is it the kind of letter I whould like to receive if I were in the reader's place?

Part VII Reading Materials

The Globalization of Business

Globalization

For better or for worse, globalization has changed the way the world does business. Though still in its early stages, it is all but unstoppable. The challenge that businesses and individuals face is learning how to live with it, manage it, and take advantage of the benefits it offers. The International Monetary Fund(IMF) defines globalization as the growing economic interdependence of countries worldwide through increasing volume and variety of cross-border transactions in goods and services and of international capital flows, and also through the more rapid and widespread diffusion of technology.

Cross-Country, Cross-Border

The current era of globalization—the world saw a similar global business push on the eve of World War I but technology and communication restraints were obvious limitations on the scope of globalization—began shortly after the end of World War II with the victorious Western powers supporting a worldwide "open" trade and investment policy. The idea was slow to catch on.

The number of companies that now deal across borders has mushroomed, as has the volume of international trade. The International Chamber of Commerce (ICC) cites statistics that show the international trade in goods and services stands at more than US$6 trillion. Global capital flows have exploded. Foreign Direct Investment(FDI), which involves the control of businesses or property across national borders, is at an all-time high in dollar volume.

The accumulated stock of foreign direct investment was more than US$3 trillion in 1997, compared to just US$735 billion just ten years ago. Cross-border sales and purchases of bonds[①] and equities[②] by American investors have risen from the equivalent of 9 percent of gross domestic product (GDP) in 1980 to more than 170 percent in the mid-1990s. Daily foreign exchange turnover is up from US$15 billion in 1973 to US$1.5

trillion by 1995. The volume of cross-border currency transactions in London, Tokyo and New York alone was US$1.5 trillion per day in 1997—more than twice what it was just five years earlier.

Technology Rules

Technology is one reason for the globalization phenomenon. Computers, which have eased telecommunication burdens, are cheaper now than they have ever been and more powerful, too. In fact, the cost of computers has fallen on average 17 percent a year over the past twenty years even while processing power has increased dramatically. One example of their impact on global communications: A one-minute telephone call from New York to London was US$300 (in 1996 dollars) in 1930. Today it costs all of one dollar. New technology will lead to even further global business integration, as the Internet becomes more accepted as a business medium worldwide.

Technology has helped small and medium-sized companies take advantage of the new markets that globalization presents. It is these companies, unencumbered by large head offices and bureaucracies that can exploit global niche markets. Computers, faxes and E-mails have replaced large parts of the traditional office structures. Smaller companies can operate more efficiently on a much wider geographical basis with less overhead than ever before. The only barrier is the imagination of the entrepreneur.

Market Open

Those who argue that globalization is a good thing say that companies dealing on the world stage will eventually become much more efficient as they benefit from large economies of scale. Productivity will be boosted and living standards everywhere have the potential to rise as the world becomes richer and more prosperous because of globalization. There is ample evidence to support the benefits argument. According to the United Nations Development Program (UNDP), total global wealth is growing faster than populations. The UNDP estimates that in the decade of the 1990s, 500 to 600 million inhabitants of the developing world have attained income levels above the poverty line and over the next 30 years another two billion should do likewise. Also, between 1965 and the early 1990s, the number of manufacturing and service industry jobs in both the developing world and the industrial world has more than doubled to 1.3 billion. And things should get even better as China, with a population of 1.2 billion or one in every five inhabitants on Earth, opens itself to the global market economy. The fall of the Soviet bloc and economic liberalization in India has already brought an additional 1.5 billion people to the global consumer marketplace.

Global Quality

The naysayers take the opposite view, claiming that globalization has, in effect, triggered a "race to the bottom." Countries with low wages are attracting jobs from higher wage-paying nations, thus dragging everyone down to their level. The alleged "exportation of jobs" has surfaced as an important political issue in most industrialized countries. Nike, the US-based sneaker manufacturer, has been raked over the coals for paying Vietnamese 84 cents an hour to make US$100 sneakers. In France, the issue has been a hot button in several parliamentary elections in the 1990s with unions claiming that upwards of 30 to 40 percent of France's more than 3 million unemployed were the victims of such "job exportation." In reality the number is less than 10 percent and most of those were in inefficient government-subsidized industries that could not adapt to global competition.

Globalization creates more jobs than it actually destroys, but they are in different sectors and in different geographic regions. It takes more skill, education and mobility to be employable. The jobs lost in Europe and North America over the decades have generally been those requiring relatively uneducated workers. Indeed, wage differentials③ between the skilled and unskilled will likely increase. Both sides can point to ample examples to support their cases. But in the end, both are probably exaggerating to some extent. What is irrefutable④ is that the world economic pie is indeed bigger because of globalization and it is being sliced differently than before.

Notes
① purchase of bonds 购买证券
② equity *n.* 股票，普通股
③ wage differential 工资差别
④ irrefutable *adj.* 无可辩驳的，驳不倒的

 Questions

1. How does technology help push the globalization of business?
2. Do you think people in both developed countries and developing countries can benefit from the globalization?

Chapter Two

Channels of Establishing Business Relations

Part I Introduction

It goes without saying that no business relations, no business. Then how and where can people find the prospective customers? A complete business deal usually involves many parties, which include producer, exporter, banks, customs, shipping company, freight, importer and consumer. The following channels can be helpful:

1. Advertisements in newspapers, televisions, magazines, or printed on the products themselves;
2. The introduction from friends, other business connections;
3. Some business websites, like E-bay and Alibaba;
4. Exhibitions both at home and abroad;
5. Import and export fairs;
6. Customer's self-introduction;
7. The Commercial Counselor's Office.

As for the credit and integrity of the merchants, it's secure to consult the banks who can make a credit investigation for you. Here are some tips for writing letters of establishing business relations:

- Write the sources of your information including the name and address, business scope, etc.;
- Make a self-introduction including your scope of business, credit and integrity;
- Tell your intention and requests;
- Expect a cooperation and early reply.

Part II Sample Letters

Sample 1 Self-Introduction

Dear Sirs,

We are honored to seek an opportunity of doing business with your prestigious organization. To further explore the possibility, I would like to give a brief description of our field.

Chapter Two

Our company is Eternal Creations Limited located in the heart of Nigeria's industrial, commercial and business center Lagos with an estimated population of over 7,000,000. We are an indigenous business firm with primary interest in consulting, marketing, distribution, international sales and manufacturers representation, franchising, publishing, travel and tours in the sub-Saharan Africa market.

The Board of Directors of our organization has resolved, as part of our diversification objective, to seek out international business partners, eager to launch its brands and products in Africa and particularly in Nigeria for maximum brand name and product exposure in this new emerging local and regional market.

We are particularly interested in discussing the possibility of representing your company domestically and regionally as Sales Representative, Independent Sales Rep., Distributor, Agent or Partner. We need not buttress the potentials of investments in the African and Nigerian markets as such information will be easily assessable to you.

We are, however, impressed of our ability, credentials and marketing capabilities to assist global companies in facilitating and promoting international business development, through sales representation using our marketing and business expertise through our local network of affiliates in Nigeria where we have particularly strong experience and an extensive network of business associates and contacts.

We look forward to a mutually beneficial relationship, as we can help reap the benefits of the global economy and achieve success in partnerships and business synergy.

Yours Truly,

Notes
1. Nigeria 尼日利亚
2. Lagos 拉各斯（尼日利亚首都）
3. We are an indigenous business firm with primary interest in consulting, marketing, distribution, international sales and manufacturers representation, franchising, publishing, travel and tours in the sub-Saharan Africa market.
   我们是一家本地公司，主要兴趣有咨询、市场营销、分销、国际销售和制造商代理、特许经营、出版、旅游，经营区域覆盖撒哈拉沙漠南部国家。
4. the Board of Directors 董事会
5. ...launching its new brands and products in Africa and particularly in Nigeria for maximum brand name and product exposure in this new emerging local and regional market.
   在非洲，尤其是尼日利亚发布自己的新品牌和产品，以期在新兴的地域和城市把品牌做大，提高产品知名度。
6. We are particularly interested in discussing the possibility of representing your company domestically and regionally as Sales Representative, Independent Sales Rep., Distributor, Agent or Partner.
   我们非常想知道自己能否成为贵公司在尼日利亚国内和地区的销售代表、独家销售代理、分销商、代理人或者合作伙伴。
7. We need not buttress the potentials of investments in the African and Nigerian markets...
我们无需强调非洲和尼日利亚市场的投资潜能……
8. ...using our marketing and business expertise through our local network of affiliates in Nigeria...
通过我们在尼日利亚的地方关系，使用我们的市场和商业资源……
9. credentials *n.* 资格，资质等级
10. synergy *n.* 共同作用，合力，协力

Sample 2 To a Potential Client Following up on Meeting

Dear Brian Johnson,

Thank you for taking the time to meet with me yesterday. I enjoyed our discussion and took careful note of your requirements in selecting business partners.

I believe very strongly that our company, a global leader in consumer electronics can provide you with the level of service you expect and deserve, and that we can establish a solid relationship with you. I welcome the opportunity to be of service to you in any way whatsoever, and look forward to meeting with you again.

I would be pleased to set up a lunch with my colleagues, as well as yourself and any colleagues you would like to bring along.

Thank you again for your time and consideration.

Sincerely,

Notes
1. a global leader in consumer electronics 一家全球领先的家用电子产品制造商
2. I would be pleased to set up a lunch with my colleagues, as well as yourself and any colleagues you would like to bring along.
我计划与同事举行午餐会，欢迎您和您的同事参加。

Sample 3 Approaching the Recommended Customers

Dear Sirs,

Your firm has been recommended to us by John Morris & Co., with whom we have done business for many years.

We specialize in the exportation of Chinese Chemicals and Pharmaceuticals, which have enjoyed great popularity in the world market. We enclose a copy of our catalogue for your reference and hope that you would contact us if any item is of interest to you. We hope you will give us an early reply.

Yours faithfully,

Notes
1. specialize in 专门（从事），专门（经营）
    We specialize in the import and export of Arts and Crafts.
    我们专门经营工艺品的进出口。
2. chemicals *n.* 化工产品，化学制品
3. pharmaceutical *n.* 药品，药剂，成药
4. enjoy great popularity 享有知名度
    类似的表达方法有：
    The goods are most popular with our customers.
    The goods have commanded a good market.
    The goods are selling very fast (or enjoy fast sales).
    The goods are universally acknowledged.
    The goods are unanimously acclaimed by our customers.

Sample 4 Introducing a Business Partner

Dear Mr. Nelson,

It is my pleasure to introduce Lily Lee, an administrative assistant of Maersk Line, China. Miss Lee is going to visit Singapore during February 2012.

This being her first visit to Singapore, she may need some guidance and business advice. I shall be highly obliged if you can spare some time to be with her and extend help during her stay over there. I believe there are mutual grounds of business interest between yours and Miss Lee's, which you may jointly explore during her visit.

I really appreciate your help.

Yours sincerely,

Notes
1. an administrative assistant 行政助理
2. Maersk Line, China 马士基（中国）有限公司，世界知名船务公司
3. be highly obliged 非常感激

Sample 5 Recommending Software

Dear Paul,

Software

From E-bay, we learn that you are in the market for Software. Our lines are predominantly Software. We wish to enter into business contract by the commencement of some practical transactions. To give you a general idea of the various kinds of Software now being available for export, we are enclosing herewith a catalogue and a price list for your examination.

Should you find interest in our items, please let us know. We shall be pleased to give you our lowest quotations upon receipt of your detailed requirements. In our trades with merchants of various countries, we always adhere to the principle of equality and mutual benefit. It is our hope to promote, by joint efforts, both trade and friendship to our mutual advantage.

We look forward to your specific enquiries with keen interest.

Yours faithfully,

Notes
1. enter into 开始（某种关系，事业，谈判等），缔结（契约等）
   We expect to enter into business talks with them next week.
   我们预计下周与他们洽谈。
   We wish to enter into business relations with your corporation for the supply of light industrial products.
   我们愿与贵公司建立贸易关系，以便取得轻工产品的供货。
2. handle *v.* 经营
   This firm handles paper and stationary.
   这家商号经营纸张文具。
   类似的说法还有：
   This firm deals in paper and stationary.
   This firm trades in paper and stationary.
   This firm is in the paper and stationary line.
3. upon receipt of 收到后……即……
   Upon receipt of your instructions, we will send the goods.
   一俟收到你方指示，我们即刻发货。
4. line *n.* 行业
   We have been in the chemical line for many years.
   我们经营化工产品已经多年了。
   be in the line=be in the field

5. in compliance with = comply with; according to 遵从，依照
   In compliance with your request, we are sending you the samples.
   应你方要求，现寄去所要样品。
6. adhere to 坚持
   We always adhere to our commitments.
   我们一贯忠实履行我们的义务。
   They choose to adhere to their views.
   他们坚持自己的观点。

Part III Reading Materials

Language

Language is a central element in communication. It may pose a barrier if its use obscures[①] meaning and distorts[②] intent. Although English is the international language of aviation[③], it is not the international language of business. Where the native languages of supervisors and employees differ, the risk of barriers to communication exists. Less obvious are subtle[④] distinctions in dialects within the same language, which may cause confusion and miscommunication. For example, the word *lift* means an elevator in Great Britain and a ride in the United States. In a different vein[⑤], there are language barriers created across disciplines and professional boundaries by the technical terminology[⑥].

Acronyms may be very useful to those on the inside of a profession or discipline as means of shorthand communication. Technical terms can convey precise meaning between professionals. However, acronyms[⑦] and technical terms may only serve to confuse, obscure, and derail[⑧] any attempt at clear understanding for people unfamiliar with their meaning and usage. Use simple, direct, declarative language. Speak in brief sentences and use terms or words you have heard from your audience. As much as possible, speak in the language of the listeners. Therefore, do not use jargon or technical language except with those who clearly understand it.

A country's language is the part of its culture. If a person is to work extensively with any one culture, it is imperative[⑨] to learn the language. Why? Because the words of the language are concepts reflecting the culture where he or she lives. As representatives or agents of companies, they must understand the language when they want to communicate with political leaders, employees, and customers. In a real sense, a language defines[⑩] a culture; thus, if a country has several spoken languages, it has several cultures. Belgium has two national languages, French in the South and Flemish[⑪] in the North. There are political and social differences between the two language groups. Canada is also a country with two formal languages—English and French. Many African and Asian nations have a far larger number of languages and cultural groups. So, marketing explorers must understand the importance of developing markets internationally.

Notes

① obscure *v.* 使朦胧，遮掩
② distort *v.* 弄歪，扭曲，曲解
③ aviation *n.* 航空学；飞行
④ subtle *adj.* 微妙的
⑤ vein *n.* 情绪
⑥ terminology *n.* 术语
⑦ acronym *n.* 首字母缩略词
⑧ derail *v.* 使……出轨
⑨ imperative *adj.* 迫切的
⑩ define *v.* 阐述，说明
⑪ Flemish *n.* 佛兰芒语（属于日耳曼语族）

> 语言是人类交际的工具，经商是离不开语言交流的。国与国、地区与地区之间都有语言差异及语言障碍问题，所以开拓国际市场者必须重视语言的学习。现在中国商人大部分靠翻译与外商打交道，有时因为翻译错误或翻译不得体而影响生意，老板却还被蒙在鼓里。比如，有许多外销员与外商谈生意时说"Our product price is very cheap."老外想cheap的product一定是bad quality，否则high quality怎能cheap呢？于是这单生意没谈成。如果说low price，外商就可接受了。恐怕因语言表达不出正确含义而痛失商机的情况数不胜数。

Questions

1. On which occasion are acronyms and technical terms best used?
2. Why is it better to learn the language of a country where one works?

Exercises

I. Fill in the blanks with the appropriate word or phrase from the following choices:

advise	be in the market for	appreciate	appreciate it	basis
buy	cover	handle	inform	meet
mutually	requirements	trade with		

1. Will you _____ a fountain pen this coming Sunday?
2. We would like to _____ you at a number of our clients _____ Chinese walnut meat.
3. Please _____ at what price your clients will place orders with us.
4. If you will send us a catalogue by air, we shall _____ very much.
5. We desire to establish _____ beneficial business relations.
6. We shall do our best to _____ your _____.
7. It is our foreign trade policy to _____ foreign countries on the _____ of

equality and mutual benefit.
8. Our corporation _____ exclusively the import and export business of light industrial products.
9. We are sending you under separate _____ two catalogues and a price list of our chemical products.
10. We _____ your sending us a special offer for walnut meat.

II. Fill in the blanks with the best choice:
1. We are sending you the samples _____ requested.
    a. be   b. are
    c. as   d. for
2. We trust that you will find our goods _____.
    a. attracting   b. to be attractive
    c. attract your attention   d. attractive
3. We would _____ very much if you send us some samples immediately.
    a. thank you   b. appreciate it
    c. appreciate   d. appreciate you
4. If any of the items is _____ to you, please let us know.
    a. interest   b. interesting
    c. interested   d. interests
5. We are _____ a copy of our catalogue for your reference.
    a. send   b. covering
    c. closed   d. enclosing
6. Our products enjoy _____ in the world market.
    a. most popular   b. great popularity
    c. good seller   d. selling fast
7. We are anxious to _____ the market for our Antimony Trioxide, which at present enjoys a limited sale in Europe.
    a. increase   b. enlarge
    c. expand   d. mutual benefit
8. We are sure that both of our companies will benefit from the joint venture and we believe this transaction will prove _____.
    a. satisfied   b. satisfy
    c. satisfactory   d. satisfied
9. We would like to take this _____ to establish business relations with you.
    a. opening   b. opportunity
    c. step   d. advantage
10. As _____ machine tools, we regret we are not in a position to supply at the moment.
    a. regard   b. regarding
    c. regards   d. retard

III. Choose the best answers:
1. Your prompt (reply, response, attention) to this matter will be greatly appreciated.

2. We have concluded considerable business with Biddle and Sawyer Company (in, of, regarding) this line of business.

3. (Provide, If, In case) you find our products (interesting, interested) to you, please let us have your specific (order, estimate, enquiry).

4. Being (specialized, handled) in the import and export of Art and Crafts, we express our desire to trade (with, to) you in this line.

5. It is (gratifying, grateful) to learn that you are in a position to supply us with Bitter Apricot Kernels.

6. To acquaint you (of, with) our products, we are sending you (by, under) separate airmail a copy of our catalogue and several sample books for your reference.

7. As to our business and (finances, financing), please refer (with, to) the Bank of Barkley, London.

8. In (comply, compliance) with your request, we sent you this morning 3 samples of our computer disks.

9. We take the liberty (in, of, to) writing you with a hope to get your best offers for Chinese carpets.

10. If your price is (in, of, with) line with the market price, we'll take large quantities.

IV. Complete the following sentences in English:

1. We are given to understand that _____.
   a. 你公司是经营化工产品的国营公司
   b. 你公司有意在平等互利的基础上与我公司建立业务关系

2. We are desirous of _____.
   a. 获得你方最近供应出口的商品目录
   b. 把你的新产品介绍给我方客户

3. Please do not hesitate to write us _____.
   a 关于推销中国水果和干果的任何建议
   b 当你方需要订购中国板栗的时候

4. As you know, _____.
   a. 我们是出口棉花的基地
   b. 我公司是信誉卓著的照相机进口商,而且愿意与你公司建立业务关系
   c. 我们已经和世界上100多个国家的商号建立了贸易关系

5. On the basis of equality, mutual benefit and exchange of needed goods, we are appreciative of _____.
   a. 你方有和我公司建立贸易关系的意图
   b. 你公司愿意到广交会来谈业务

6. We hope you can provide us with _____.
   a. 中国制造的电子手表2000只
   b. 中国制造的山地车300辆

7. We are glad that in the past few years _____
   我们之间通过双方努力在业务上和友谊上都有很大改进

8. Upon receipt of your specific enquiries, _____.
   我们即办理一切必要的事宜

9. Your price is too high, and _____.

a. 我们恐怕达不成协议
   b. 我们无法销售您的产品
10. It would be very nice _____.
    假如您能将你们开发的软件详情告知我方

V. Translate the following into English:

1. 为了让您对我方的各类出口纺织品有个大体了解，随信寄上样本和价格单，供您参阅。
2. 本地的中国银行国外业务部推荐你公司与中国公司建立贸易关系，以推销你们的轻工业产品。
3. 我们有一客户想购买中国红茶。
4. 我们得知你方出口中国工艺品，特此与您联系。
5. 如果你们能及时报盘，我们相信我们能尽力说服我方客户接受。
6. 如果你方认为我们的报价可行，请即来信，以便我方报确盘。
7. 付款以不可撤销的信用证，凭即期汇票付款。
8. 我公司是该地区电子产品的主要进口商之一。我们借此机会与贵方接洽，希望与贵方建立贸易关系。
9. 有关我们的资信情况，请向中国银行上海分行查询。
10. 据悉你方是日用化学品制造商。我们有一客户想要购买贵国化妆品，如能立即航寄样品，将不胜感激。

VI. Letter writing:

Practice writing a letter for Establishing Business Relationship which should cover the following details:

1. The source of information: Chamber of Commerce;
2. Self-introduction: having been handling textiles for many years;
3. Desire: to establish business relationship on the basis of equality and mutual benefit;
4. Sending catalogue and pamphlets for reference;
5. Ready to make a quotation upon inquiry.

Chapter Three

Enquiries and Replies

Part I Introduction

Enquiry means asking for information about certain products by the buyers or importers. It can be made by letters, e-mails, cables, fax, telex or even face-to-face talk. There are general enquiries and specific enquiries. In a general enquiry, the general information is wanted about some goods, but not an immediate business; while in a specific enquiry, business is meant to be done right away if the offer is acceptable. The contents of an enquiry can cover price, specifications, quality, quantity, packing, delivery, catalogues, samples and sample books.

The following points are helpful in sending a successful enquiry:
- Be polite in your tone and diction;
- Keep it short and to the point;
- Make it initiative enough to have the recipient reply to you as soon as possible.

The outline of an enquiry:
- Introduce your firm and your products;
- State the purpose of your letter, telex, fax, or call;
- Explain what you want the reader to do;
- Give an exact description or specification of the products you want covering the weight, material, quantity, delivery, size;
- Make clear the terms, methods of payment, and discount you expect;
- Give an optimistic ending and wish an early reply.

Part II Sample Letters

Sample 1 Enquiry for Rubber & Tire

Dear Sirs,

We learned from Canton Fair, Guangzhou, that you are a leading rubber & tire machinery supplier in your country, committed to the R&D and innovation of informatization equipment, providing an integrated solution and equipment with the combination of software and hardware, management and control.

We are, at present, very much interested in importing your goods and would appreciate your sending us catalogues, sample books or even samples if possible.

Please give us detailed information CIF Qingdao prices, discounts, and terms of payment. We hope this will be good start for our long and profitable business relations.

Truly yours,

Notes
1. a leading rubber & tire machinery supplier 橡胶轮胎机械设备的一家主要供货商
2. Canton Fair, Guangzhou 广交会
3. R & D = research and development 研发
4. ...committed to the R&D and innovation of informatization equipment, providing an integrated solution and equipment with the combination of software and hardware, management and control.
……致力于信息化装备的研发与创新，为橡胶轮胎企业提供软硬件结合、管控一体的成套装备及完整解决方案。
5. CIF = Cost, Insurance and Freight 保险，成本加运费

Sample 2   The Reply

Dear Sirs,

We welcome you for your inquiry dated June 12 and thank you for your interest in our export of Rubber & Tires. We are enclosing some copies of our illustrated catalogues and price list giving the details you asked for. Also under separate cover, we are sending you some samples, which will show you clearly the quality and craftsmanship. We trust that when you see them you will agree that our products appeal to the most selective buyer.

We allow a proper discount according to the quantity ordered. As to terms of payment, we usually require Letter of Credit payable by sight draft.

Thank you again for your interest in our products. We are looking forward to your order and you may be assured that it will receive our prompt and careful attention.

Truly yours,

Notes
1. under separate cover = by separate post, by separate mail 另封邮寄
We are sending you catalogues under separate cover.
=We are sending you catalogues by separate mail.
我方为你方另封邮寄产品目录。

under cover 随函附寄
We are sending you under cover a copy of our price list.
我们随函附寄价格单一份。
2. quality and craftsmanship 质量与工艺

Sample 3 Enquiring for Textiles

Dear Sirs,

Messrs Jones & Smith of New York informed us that you are exporters of all cotton bed-sheets and pillowcases. We would like you to send us details of your previous ranges, including sizes, colors and prices, and also samples of the different qualities of materials used.

We are large dealers in textiles and believe there is a promising market in our area for moderately priced goods of this kind mentioned above.

When quoting, please state your terms of payment and discount you would allow on purchases of quantities of not less than 100 dozen of individual items. Prices quoted should include insurance and freight to Liverpool.

We are looking forward to your early reply.

Yours faithfully,

Notes
1. bed-sheets 床单
   color-checked bed-sheets 彩格床单
   color-striped bed-sheets 彩条床单
2. range n. 行，列；（一）种，（一）类；范围，区域，界限；差距
   a full range of samples 一整套样品
   a full range of shipping documents 一整套装运单据
   a wide range of designs 各种款式
   a narrow range of prices 很小的价格差距
   the range of business activities 经营范围
3. discount n. 折扣；贴现；减价
   The highest discount we can allow on this article is 10%.
   我们对这项商品最多只能打九折。
   The rate of discount in London is now 5%.
   现在伦敦的贴现率是5%。
   at a discount 折扣，贴水，低于正常价格；没有销路，容易到手
   Many articles are reported to be selling at a discount.
   据报道，许多商品在打折销售。
   Off-grade qualities are now at a discount.
   等外品没有销路。

Sample 4   The Reply

Dear Sirs,

We are very pleased to receive your enquiry of 20th January and enclose our illustrated catalogue and price list giving the details you asked for. Also by separate post, we are sending you some samples and feel confident that you will agree the goods are both good in quality and reasonable in price.

For our regular purchases in quantities of not less than 100 dozen of individual items, we would allow a discount of 2%. Payment is to be made by irrevocable L/C at sight.

Because of their softness and durability, our all cotton bed-sheets and pillowcases are rapidly becoming popular. If you place your order not later than the end of this month, we can ensure prompt shipment.

We would also very much like to invite your attention to our other products such as table-cloth and table napkins, details of which you will find in the catalogue and we are looking forward to receiving your first order.

Yours faithfully,

Notes

1. invite one's attention to 提请某人注意,
   类似表达还有:
   call one's attention to
   draw one's attention to
   direct one's attention to
   We wish to call your attention to the shipment of our Order No.32.
   敬请注意我方32号订单货物的装运。
   receive one's attention 得到注意, 予以办理
   Your letter has received our careful attention.
   我们已经认真处理了你方来信。
2. order *n.* 定单, 定购, 所订货物; 汇票
   We accept the order subject to payment in advance.
   如果预付货款我们就可以接受订货。
   Please do not send any remittance until the order is confirmed.
   在未确认定单之前, 请勿将款汇来。
   在表示所订商品时, order 后一般接for, 间或接of。
   We thank you for your order of 100 tons of Bitter Apricot Kernels.
   感谢你方关于100吨苦杏仁的订单。
   order *v.* 订购, 订货

If you order immediately, we can arrange probably 5,000 cases.
如果你方能够立即下订单，我们即可安排运出5,000箱货物。
We note that you contemplate ordering 2,000 footballs at the same price as last.
我们注意到你方打算照上次价格订购足球2,000个。

Sample 5 Superior White Sugar

Dear Sirs,

We have just received an enquiry from one of our Japanese clients for 10,000 metric tons of the captioned sugar, and shall appreciate your quoting us the best price at the earliest date.

For your information, the quality required should be superior white crystal sugar packed in new gunny bags of 50kgs each. Meanwhile, the goods should be surveyed by an independent surveyor about the quality and weight before shipment. For this enquiry, the buyers will arrange shipping and insurance, therefore, the price to be quoted should be on FAS basis.

As there is a critical shortage of sugar in Japan, the goods should be ready for shipment as early as possible. Please be assured that if your price is acceptable, we will place an order with you right away.

Your early reply will be greatly appreciated.

Faithfully yours,

Notes
1. for your information or for your study 供你方参考
   For your information, the tendency of the leather market is still uncertain.
   特通知你方，皮革市场的行情仍不明了。
2. survey *n.* 检验，鉴定
   survey report 鉴定报告
   surveyor's report 鉴定机构报告
   customs surveyor 海关检验人员
   engineer surveyor 工程检验人员
   marine surveyor 海事检验人员
3. shortage *n.* 短重，所短货物
   There is a shortage of 886 kg.
   货物少运了886公斤。
   Please do your utmost to ship the shortage by the next available vessel.
   请赶最早船只装运所短重的货物。
4. FAS = Free Alongside Ship （成交术语）船边交货

5. shipment n. 装运，所运货物
   The date of shipment is August/ September.
   装运日期为8/9月份。
   We find the shipment ex Dongfeng is pretty good.
   我们认为东风轮所运来的货物很不错。

Sample 6　To Establish Direct Contact with Customers

Dear Sirs,

　　We'd like to take this opportunity to express our heartfelt thanks for the kind cooperation you extended to us over past years. We appreciate all your supports for so long time that really mean so much to us.

　　The purpose of this letter is to outline our new business strategy which has been recently determined by the management of the company. The theme of this strategy is that, instead of passively waiting for the orders from traders/brokers, we will carry out the entire marketing activities and customer services by ourselves, in order to further strengthen the customer relationships, enlarge the market shares as well as company profit. Under this new policy, from next year we will suspend all the communications with various intermediaries and start to develop business relationship with the buyers directly.

　　In support of this new strategy, we have already set up a talented, motivated and experienced sales team who is familiar with all international business practices, especially American practices very well. We do believe this sales team will exceed the level of performance the customers previously enjoyed from the traders/brokers. Moreover, with just-in-time market information and dynamic technology exchanges, flexible payment terms and value-added services, we could expect more and better mutual benefits with the customers in the future.

　　Being a most honored and treasured customer for us, we sincerely wish we could establish business relationship with your esteemed organization directly. And we do believe our above-mentioned customer focused strategy will create a long-term mutual beneficial cooperation between us.

　　We are looking forward for your favorable consideration on this matter. Should you have any questions and/or concerns, please feel free to contact me directly. I will contact you in one-week time as a follow-up to this letter.

Yours sincerely,

Notes

1. trader/broker 交易人/经纪人
   stock broker 股票经纪人
2. enlarge the market shares 扩大市场份额
3. suspend *v.* 中止，搁置
   Trade with that company was suspended for ten years.
   与那家公司的交易被中断了十年。
4. intermediary *n.* 中介机构，中间人
5. value-added serrice 增值服务

Part III Reading Materials

1. Trade Barrier Tariff

Tariff, also called duty, is a tax collected by a government on the goods imported and sometimes also on the goods exported, which is imposed on imports or exports to increase the government revenues①, to weaken the competitive power of the imported goods and for some other purposes. There are various tariffs covering Revenue Tariff, Protective Tariff, Prohibitive tariff, Retaliatory Tariff②, Regulatory Tariff, and Anti-dumping Tariff. Revenue tariff is imposed to increase the revenue income of the government, which is usually low. It is of little importance to large industrial countries but a major source of revenue in many less developed countries.

Protective Tariff is higher than the average increased value-added tax as its main purpose is to weaken the competitive power of the imported goods by raising the price of imported goods through high tax so as to protect domestic goods. If the tariff is raised so high that the imported goods in the importing country may have little margin of profits in the business transaction, then it's called Prohibitive Tariff. The Prohibitive Tariff is likely to cause retaliation from those countries which sustain losses. They will perhaps also raise their importing duty to discourage the exports of the country that has initiated the Prohibitive Tariff. This is called Retaliatory Tariff. Retaliatory Tariff is also imposed to offset the export subsidies of some other countries, in which case, it's also called Counter-subsidy tariff.

Regulatory Tariff is a kind of temporary tariff which can be carried out by the administrative bodies to reorient importation and protect some industries. But usually the tariff rates are stipulated by the legislative body of a country after going through complex processes and remain unalterable for a long period of time. Anti-dumping Tariff is a very high and punitive tax imposed on imports of dumped products sold at a very low price or even lower than the production cost or the home-country price. The government which intends to impose Anti-dumping Tariff must investigate to prove that the goods are being dumped into its territory and also must prove that the dumping causes or threatens to cause material injury to an established industry in its territory or materially retards the establishment of a domestic industry. If the dumping has been proved, the government of the importing country can levy Anti-dumping Tariff, which, however, should not be greater in amount than the margin of price caused by dumping.

Notes
① government revenues 政府税收
② Retaliatory Tariff 报复性关税

 Questions

1. How many kinds of tariffs can be placed on the import of goods?
2. What are the standards for judging the constitution of dumping?
3. Do you think trade barriers are necessary or not?

2. The Role of Culture in Business

What role does culture play and can it be a positive one? A manager in a Swedish pharmaceutical firm described what happened when a multicultural team was put together.

Product design was traditionally carried out at our Stockholm① headquarters. Once, by accident or design, we brought in an international team to discuss the design of a new allergy② product. Due to extreme differences of opinion on what constitutes③ good medical practice, the team designed the new product with maximum flexibility to suit the major demands of each country. Later, we discovered this flexibility to be of great advantage in developing and marketing international competitive products.

Regarding cultural difference as a challenge rather than a problem may mean a little more investment of time and funds, but it is more likely to produce international workable teams, systems and products. This general approach albeit④ with variances on each case, has helped Japanese, Germans and Scandinavians⑤ adapt successfully to international markets. It has also helped cultivate the deep awareness of quality and consumer-friendliness, which characterizes the products of these successful countries, and pervades⑥ business thinking and aspirations.

So if international companies are to tackle⑦ the challenge of culture, where do they start? Let us look in more details at the areas of business activity, which need to be culture-responsive. Steven Globeman discussed this issue as follows:

Culture differences do not, as a rule, prohibit doing business internationally, although they often oblige⑧ management to modify the way business is done from region to region. While modifications may be required, to a greater or lesser extent, in virtually⑨ all of the international firms' activities, the particular areas that seem to be affected by cultural differences are the marketing and personnel relation's functions.

Its points in the right direction and its implications are clear: managing and communicating with a culturally different or varied workforce requires new methods and techniques. Success in this first objective is needed so that the company may understand consumers whose behavior and tastes are different from that of the home country.

In order that culture and language may not be a constraint⑩ on international business, and indeed that they may be an asset, a company which is, or aims to be, internationally active should adopt a positive policy of adaptation. This policy comprises key points as follows:

Adaptation of the Self

The cultural imperialism associated with earlier models of international business cannot prevail⑪ in a world where the customer is king. Similarly, the expectation that native speakers of English need to make no allowance for⑫ those with no command of English language is now dangerous. The language of business is the language of the customer and anthropology has taught us that the best route to the understanding of a foreign culture is through its language.

Adaptation to Host Governments

Awareness of relevant laws, regulations, ethics and the general business environment are essential. Every company needs to ensure that its practices and products are acceptable to the target community. Cultural competence required here will be of a formal kind involving links with government agencies, banks, etc., and demanding knowledge of the local business environment.

Adaptation to Collaborators

Cultural competence⑬ will be of more informal nature. Frequent personal contact with agents, partners and the like will demand extensive language skills and background knowledge. This exposure is clearly at its importance when a full subsidiary employing members of the local population is set up. Try to consider the adaptation to collaborators, especially assumptions which should be tested.

Notes

① Stockholm *n.* 斯德哥尔摩（瑞典首都）
② allergy *n.* 过敏症；反感，厌恶
③ constitute *v.* 构成，制造
④ albeit *conj.* 纵然，即使
⑤ Scandinavian *n.* 斯堪的那维亚的
⑥ pervade *v.* 散布；弥漫
⑦ tackle *v.* 抓住，捉住（对手）；处理（问题）
⑧ oblige *v.* 强迫
⑨ virtually *adv.* 几乎，差不多
⑩ constraint *v.* 强迫；受威胁
⑪ prevail *v.* 占上风，盛行；生效
⑫ allowance for 体谅
⑬ competence *n.* 力量；能力

Questions

1. Which areas of an international company are particularly affected by cultural differences?

2. What shall a company do to turn culture and language differences into an asset?

Chapter Three

> 文化差异是种挑战，处理文化差异问题需要灵活的策略。处理好文化角色问题需要三个适应，即自我适应、对工作国政府适应、对合作者适应。这三个适应是发挥文化角色的三个基本方向。

Exercises

I. Fill in the blanks with the appropriate word from the following choices:

| accepting   acceptable   accepted   accept |

1. Your offer is not _____.
2. We regret we cannot _____ your offer.
3. We are _____ your counteroffer on condition that your order amounts to 10,000 dozen.
4. We have made our prices so low that they should be readily _____ to our customers.
5. Your offer is _____, and we are awaiting your confirmation.

II. Fill in the blanks with the best choice:

1. We thank you for your letter of May 15 and the _____ catalogue.
    a. sent   b. enclosed
    c. given   d. presented
2. The letter we sent last week is an enquiry _____ color TV sets.
    a. about   b. for
    c. of   d. as
3. This price is _____ of your 5% commission.
    a. includes   b. covering
    c. inclusive   d. including
4. _____ your Enquiry No. 12, we are sending you a catalogue and a sample book for your reference.
    a. According   b. As per
    c. As   d. About
5. No discount will be allowed _____ you could place an order for more than 5,000 pcs.
    a. unless   b. till
    c. besides   d. except
6. We expect to place a trial order _____ you in the near future.
    a. in   b. with
    c. for   d. on
7. We think it would be _____ to take in orders from those firms whose standing and financial position are yet unknown.
    a. premature   b. favorable
    b. convenient   d. desirable

8. _____ please find a price list of our new products.
   a. Enclosing   b. Enclose
   c. Enclosed   d. Encloses
9. July shipment is acceptable _____ our customer.
   a. /   b. to
   c. for   d. in
10. As requested, we are pleased to quote you without engagement the _____.
    a. follows   b. follow
    c. following   d. followed

III. Translate the following sentences into Chinese:
1. 请报给我们200公吨钢板青岛成本运费价，并告知详细规格。
2. 我们的钢笔价格是每打人民币30元船边交货价。
3. 关于支付条件，我们要求不可撤销的、凭即期汇票支付的信用证。
4. 信内附有带插图的目录一份，望查收。
5. 我们很有可能向你方订一大笔货。
6. 如果你方价格有竞争力，发货期也合适，我们就下定单。
7. 买方要求卖方一周内装运1万公吨磷酸盐。
8. 随函附上根据你方第15号询价单所开的报价单，期待你方确认。
9. 请报你方最优惠的上海到岸价，包括我方3%的佣金。
10. 谢谢你方3月16日的询价，现报盘如下：
    4000打工作手套，每打人民币40元CIF Singapore，船期8/9月份。
    我们要求不可撤消的、凭即期汇票支付的信用证。
    上述报价以我方最后确认为准。

IV. Correct the mistakes in the following sentences:
1. This will help cement at our business relation.
2. To establish business relations with you is what we have longed for years.
3. We avail this opportunity to write to you and see if we can establish business relations by a start of some practical transactions.
4. We too pleased to deal in your products.
5. We so sorry that we could not answer your letter in due time.
6. Please place order from us if you find our price competitive.
7. We shall get touch with you as soon as we have fresh supplies.
8. We are in bad need of Grade A.
9. With the view to secure orders, please send us a quotation sheet for this article.
10. We very regret our inability to make you an offer at present.

V. Letter writing:
Practice writing a letter of Inquiry which should cover the following details:
1. Self-introduction: one of the largest dealers of garments interested in ladies' dresses of all descriptions;
2. Asking for samples and quotations per dozen CIF Vancouver;
3. Attitude towards Chinese Products: have confidence;
4. An optimistic expectation: a promising market.

Chapter Four

Offers and Counteroffers

Part I Introduction

An offer is a promise to supply goods on the terms and conditions stated. In an offer, the seller not only quotes the price of the goods he wishes to sell but also indicates all necessary terms of sales for the buyer's consideration and acceptance.

An offer can be firm or non-firm.

A firm offer is made when a seller promises to sell goods at a stated price within a stated period of time. The promise may be expressed (i.e. clearly stated in words), as when it takes the form of a letter; or it may be implied (i.e. understood), as when it takes the form of a quotation that contains the words "for acceptance within seven days," or similar qualifying words. It should also state the following points clearly, such as name of the commodity, quality, specifications, quantity, packing, price, delivery date and terms of payment including invoicing, transportation and insurance.

The firm offers create a power of acceptance permitting the offeree, by accepting the offer, to transform the offeror's promise into a contractual obligation. Thus once it has been accepted, it can't be withdrawn.

The firm offers must be clear, definite, complete and final. The terms stated in a firm offer is binding on the sellers if they are accepted by the buyers within its validity. In a firm offer, an exact description of the goods, the time of shipment and the mode of payment should be included.

Non-firm offers are offers with reservation clause and are usually indicated by means of sending catalogues, pricelists, proforma invoices and quotations; though quotations with certain qualifying words sometimes play the function of firm offers. Non-firm offers are not final, often with such words as "subject to prior sale" or "subject to our final confirmation," or "an offer without engagement (obligation)."

The main differences between a firm offer and non-firm offer are: Offerors have responsibility to make deal when their partners accept all conditions in their firm offer while offerors are not responsible to make deal when their partner do this in the cases of non-firm offer. Therefore, offerors should mention in their offer which one it is, a firm offer or a non-firm offer.

A counteroffer is virtually a partial rejection of the original offer and also a counter proposal initiated by the buyer or the offeree. The buyer may show disagreement to the price, or packing, or shipment and state his own terms instead. Such alterations, no matter how slight they may appear to be, signify that business has to be negotiated on the renewed basis. The original offeror or the seller now becomes the offeree and has the full right of acceptance or refusal. In the latter case, he may make another counter offer of his own. This process can go on for many a round till business is finalized or called off. In making a counter offer, one has to state the terms most explicitly and use words very carefully so as to avoid ambiguity or misunderstanding, which is the same way as one usually does in making an offer.

Part II Sample Letters

Sample 1 A Firm Offer

Dear Sirs,

We have received your e-mail dated 13th of May from which we note that you wish to have an offer from us for 30 metric tons of Green Beans, 2012 Crop, for shipment to Qingdao.

In answer to your enquiry, subject to your reply reaching us by June 12th, Beijing time, we are making you the following offer:

"36 metric tons of Green Beans, FAQ 2012 Crop, at CNY 40,000 per metric ton CIF 3% Qingdao, shipment per steamer during June/July via Hong Kong. Other terms and conditions are the same as usual, with the exception of insurance which will cover All Risks and War Risks for 110% of the invoice value."

We await your positive reply with great interest.

Yours faithfully,

Notes
1. metric tons 公吨
2. subject to= depending on 取决于，以……为准
   This offer is firm, subject to the receipt of your reply here by the 14th of July.
   本发盘为确盘，以你方7月14日复到有效。
3. FAQ（Fair Average Quality）大路货，良好平均品质
4. shipment per steamer during June/July via Hong Kong 6月或7月份装船，经由香港
5. cover All Risks and War Risks for 110% of the invoice value
   按照发票金额的110%投保一切险和战争险

Sample 2   A Non-firm Offer

Dear Sirs,

We thank you for your enquiry of July 12 and confirm having sent an e-mail to you today in reply, as per confirmation copy enclosed. As requested, we are also sending you, by S.F. Express with the tracking number 574066743464 one catalogue and two sample books for our Shanghai printed pure silk fabrics. We hope they will reach you in due course and will help you in making your selection.

In order to start a concrete transaction between us, we take pleasure in making you a special offer, subject to our final confirmation, as follows:

Article No.: 9001 Yunnan
Design No.: 72435-2A
Specification: 20×30
Colors: white, blue, green and yellow
Minimum: 30,000 yards
Packing: in wooden cases
Unit Price: US$ 20 per yard CIFC 3%
Shipment: August/September, 2012
Terms of Payment: by 100% confirmed, irrevocable letter of credit payable by draft at sight to be opened 30 days before the time of shipment.

This offer is firm, subject to your reply here by 17th July.

Yours faithfully,

Notes
1. as per = according to 根据，参见
2. enclosed 所附的
   as per confirmation copy enclosed: 内容如所附抄件
3. S.F. Express 顺风快递
4. tracking number 订单查询号码
5. catalogue 商品目录
6. sample books 样品册
7. in due course 如期地，在适当的时候
   We trust the shipment will reach you in due course.
   我们相信船货将如期到达。
   But Apple should be able to correct such flaws in due course.
   但苹果公司应该会有能力及时修正这样的瑕疵。
8. Article No. = Item No. 货号
9. By 100% confirmed, irrevocable letter of credit payable by draft at sight to be opened

30 days before the time of shipment. 以保兑的、不可撤销的即期信用证付款，信用证须于装船前30天开出。

Sample 3 A Counter Offer

Dear Sirs,

We are in receipt of your letter of 5th July, offering us 200 metric tons of Groundnuts, hand-picked, shelled and non-graded at CNY 5,000 net per metric ton CFR Copenhagen or any other EMP for shipment during October/November, 2012.

In reply, we regret to inform you that our buyers find your price is rather on the high side. Information indicates that some parcels of Indian origin have been sold here at a level about 10% lower than yours.

We do not deny that the quality of Chinese kernels is slightly better, but the difference in price should, in no case, be as big as 10%. To step up the trade, we counter-offer as follows, subject to your reply received by us on or before 20th July:

  50 metric tons of groundnut kernels FAQ 2012 crop
  at RMB 4,500 per m/t CIF Rotterdam,
  other terms as per your letter of 5th July

As the market is declining, we recommend your immediate acceptance.

Yours faithfully,

Notes
 1. hand-picked, shelled and non-graded 手工挑选、去壳、不分级别的
 2. EMP European Main Ports 欧洲主要港口
 3. CFR Cost and Freight 成本加运费
 4. origin *n.* 产地
  country of origin 生产国别，原产地
  Certificate of Origin 原产地证

Sample 4 Counter-offer on Price of Silk Scarves

Dear Sirs,

Thanks very much for your offer No. 25 offering us 2,000 pieces of embroidered Silk Scarves at US$30 per piece CIF New York.

Our customers are interested in the fine quality and beautiful designs of your products.

However, they thought the quotation is much on the high side, i.e. 10% higher than the average. They insisted that they place larger orders provided that your price is reduced to about US$ 25 per piece. It means a good chance of concluding a bigger transaction with them if you can meet their requirements. We sincerely hope you can take the advantage of this opportunity to expand your sales.

We await your positive reply with great interest.

Yours faithfully,

Notes
1. embroidered silk scarves 绣花丝绸披肩
2. design *n.* 设计，图样，花样，款式；*v.* 设计
   We have various designs of Machine Printed Rayon Sateen available for export at the moment.
   我方目前有多种图案的丝贡缎可供出口。
   Our silverware enjoy a great popularity in European market due to its delicate design and superior quality.
   我们的银器设计精致，质量上乘，在欧洲市场十分畅销。

Sample 5 Counter-offer on Payment Terms

Dear Sirs,

We thank you for your quotation of April 23, 2012 for 600 Hisense 3100 Color TV sets. We find your price as well as delivery date satisfactory. However, we would suggest you alter the payment terms.

Our past purchase of other household electrical appliances from you has been paid as a rule by confirmed, irrevocable letter of credit at sight. On this basis, it has indeed cost us a great deal. From the moment of opening credit till the time our buyers pay us, the tie up of our funds lasts about four months. At present, this problem is particularly taxing owing to the tight financial condition and the high bank interest.

In view of our long business relations and our prospective future cooperation, we suggest that you accept either "Cash against Documents on arrival of goods" or "Drawing on us at 60 days' sight".

Your first priority to the consideration of the above request and early favorable reply will be highly appreciated.

Yours faithfully,

Notes
1. tie up of one's funds 资金占用
2. taxing *adj.* 难以负担的，使人感到有压力的
   Such an amount is taxing to a medium-sized firm.
   这样一笔数额对一个中等财力的商号来说是有压力的。
3. tight *adj.* 紧张的，短缺的
   tight money 资金短缺
   tight-up of funds 占用资金
   cash against documents on arrival of goods 货到后凭单付款
4. drawing on us at 60 days' sight 开出见票60天付款的汇票向我们收款
   draw *v.* 开出
   draw a draft 开汇票
   draw (a draft) on sb. for …… 开出向某人收款的汇票
   As agreed, we are drawing a draft on you for the value of this sample shipment.
   按照商定，我们对所购样货开汇票索款。
   drawings *n. (pl.)* 用汇票支取的金额
   Your letter of credit is to allow 5% more or less drawings.
   你方信用证应准许在收款时有5%的上下幅度。
5. priority *n.* 优先
   top priority/ first priority 最优先
   We'll give first priority to your orders.
   我们将最优先考虑你方的订单。
   The question of payment will take top priority in our discussions.
   支付问题是我们优先探讨的问题。
   You may enjoy priority in our offers.
   你方可在我方报盘方面享有优先权。

Sample 6 Declining an Offer

Dear Sirs,

We thank you for your order of July 3 for 100 Mountain Bikes. We regret to say, however, we could do nothing but save it as a temporary file for our future reference. It's impossible for us to accept new orders due to the fact that there is an urgent demand of our bikes both at home and abroad. Due to the recent energy crisis, orders from European buyers have been on a constant rise.

We express our deepest regret for being unable to accept your order. However, we are sure to contact you immediately should the situation improve.

Yours faithfully,

Notes

1. save it as a temporary file for future reference 将其暂时存档，以供将来参考
2. there is an urgent demand of 对……的需求甚殷
3. should the situation improve 一旦情况好转

Part III Reading Materials

Tariff Barriers and Non-tariff Trade Barriers (NTBs)

A tariff is a tax or duty levied on commodities when they cross national boundaries, normally an import duty, for the purpose of raising their selling price in the importing nation's market to reduce competition against domestic producers. It is the most common method of restricting trade. Tariffs may be barely placed on exports, because they want to encourage exports. A tariff may be one of the following four kinds: ad valorem①, specific, alternative②, or compound③. An ad valorem, most commonly used, is figured as a percentage on the value of goods—for example, 10, 20 or 25 percent. They may be based, depending on the country, either on the value of the goods landed at the port of destination, or at the port in the country of origin. A specific duty relates to local currency per unit of goods based on weight, number, length, volume, or other unit of measurement—for example, US$25 per pound or per yard. An alternative duty is where either an ad valorem duty or a specific one can be prescribed for a product, with the requirement that the more exertive one shall apply. A compound duty is a combination of an ad valorem duty and a specific one—for example, 10 percent of value plus US$1 per kilogram.

Tariffs have the advantage that they can be selectively levied in terms of products and with differential rates. Therefore, a country may attain rather precise objectives with tariffs while increasing government revenues at the same time. The negative respect of tariffs is that they increase the cost of imports to the customers.

Contrary to tariff duties which are relatively transparent, non-tariff barriers are often more complex and difficult to sniff and therefore assess than tariffs, because they can be "hidden" in rules and practices that have a perfectly legitimate objective. Furthermore, non-tariff barriers can have more trade–restrictive effects than tariffs, which raise the cost of a given product and go as far as excluding a good from a market altogether. Known as "green trade barriers," new non-tariff barriers to trade, such as technical trade barriers and environmental trade barriers, have tended to take the place of traditional trade barriers.

Notes

① ad valorem duty 从价税
② alternative duty 选择税
③ compound duty 复合关税

 **Questions**

1. What is a tariff and what is it supposed to do?
2. What are the advantages and disadvantages of trade tariffs?
3. What are the differences between tariff barriers and NTBs?

Culture Notes
Cultural Conflicts in Marketing

In order to export its products, an international corporation has to make marketing strategies and has them carried out. Marketing is one of the important elements for an exporter to compete and survive.

Cultural conflicts may occur in international marketing. Great attention must be paid to this. Basically, exporters encounter culture at two distinct levels:

- The individual level: At this level, they negotiate and communicate with their direct contacts in the market.
- The market level: At this level, they satisfy the needs of their customers by modifying products and approaches to appeal to the population at large. Despite the influence of one on the other, anticipating individual behavior premised entirely on the inclinations of society is to deny the strong influence of one's family, profession, social class, generation and many other influences. In the same way, anticipating market behavior based on single individual is equally spurious, as the collective experience of the society might bear little resemblance to the model.

Cultural Conflicts in Business Administration

Cultural conflicts often occur in the administration of an international company where employees are from different cultures. As more and more investment goes to foreign countries, the number of subsidiaries, joint ventures and other affiliated businesses is increasing worldwide. Those businesses include people from different cultures at all levels. Especially the senior managers might be made up of mixed cultures. In an international company, the general manager may come from the UK where headquarters of the company are located, the sales manager may be from the host country, and the accounting manager may come from Japan. These managers may find themselves encountering conflicts resulting from culture. Besides, the foreign managers may likewise encounter cultural conflicts when they deal with problems with employees.

Cultural Conflicts in Business Public Relations

The process of doing business is actually an art of how to deal with the relationship between people. This is especially true of doing international business because more than one culture is involved in the whole process. A businessman who is expert at dealing with public relations is more likely to succeed. But, when he is in a strange culture or when he is dealing with public relations linked to different cultures, he has to be careful with the cultural conflicts. It is quite likely for a man who is not familiar with the cultural conflicts to offend other people before he can realize it.

Chapter Four

Notes

① premised ... on/upon 根据，基于……
② spurious *adj.* 假的，伪造的
③ subsidiary *adj.* 辅助的，附属公司
④ affiliated *adj.* 隶属的
⑤ offend *v.* 得罪，冒犯

 Questions

1. At what distinct levels may exporters encounter cultural conflicts?
2. Why could there be cultural conflicts in business admistration?
3. What can be the influences of cultural conflicts in business public relations?

Exercises

I. Fill in the blanks with proper words or expressions.

1. As the market is declining, your price is rather on the _____ side.
2. Since your price is _____ with the present market, it is not workable for the market at our end.
3. In _____ to your letter, we are making the following offer.
4. Our offer is firm, _____ to our final confirmation.
5. The insurance is to be _____ by the buyer.
6. We offer you 200 tons of "Style" brand Newsprint at US$2,200 _____ ton on the usual terms.
7. We _____ your favorable reply by the end of this month.
8. We assure you that the goods will reach you in _____.
9. In view of our long-term relationship, we take _____ in making you a special offer.
10. It means a good chance of _____ a bigger transaction between us.

II. Fill in the blanks with the best choice:

1. When the seller pays for the goods to be loaded on board the containership, but does not pay the freight or insurance, the right term is _____.
   a. FOB　　　b. FCA　　　c. CFR　　　d. CIF
2. When the seller pays for all the charges up to the port of shipment including the loading of a consignment on board the carrying vessel, the term is _____.
   a. CIF　　　b. FOB　　　c. CFR　　　d. DDP
3. When the seller undertakes to pay for the cost of transport in the case of container delivery of the goods to a specified destination, as well as for the cost of insuring them while in transit, and he includes these charges in his sales price, the term is _____.
   a. DAP　　　b. CIP　　　c. CPT　　　d. CFR

4. What is the term when the consignment is delivered with all the charges up to arrival at the place of destination paid by the seller? _____.
   a. FOB   b. CFR   c. DDP   d. CIF
5. When the seller pays for the goods to be placed alongside the vessel on the quay or in lighters at the named port of shipment, the term is _____.
   a. DAT   b. FAS   c. FOB   d. EXW
6. We would make you the following offer, subject to your cable acceptance _____ us not later than Sept. 20, 2004.
   a. reaches   b. being reached
   c. reaching   d. reach
7. The design of the carpets is very nice and could definitely _____ the requirements of our customers.
   a. attract   b. appeal
   c. meet   d. please
8. Enclosed herewith are our catalogue and some samples for your _____.
   a. request   b. review
   c. reply   d. reference
9. Now the problem is quite _____ owing to a tight money condition on our side.
   a. necessary   b. taxing
   c. hard   d. acceptable
10. In view of the fact that our _____ on hand has been quite low owing to heavy commitment, your early order is absolutely essential.
    a. opportunity   b. stock
    c. delivery   d. shipment

III. Translate the following sentences into English:
1. 我们正在仔细研究你方报盘，希望将此盘有效期保留到月底。
2. 如果你方能订购3,000打或3,000打以上，我们将给予10%的折扣。
3. 由于原料价格上涨幅度较大，很抱歉不能接受你方报盘。
4. 按照你们的要求，我们报50公吨大豆的实盘如下，以本日起一周内你方复到有效。
5. 如果首次船货的质量使我们客户满意，我们相信你们会从他们那里获得更多的订单。
6. 我们相信你方很容易销售我们的女装，因为我们的女装在你方市场早已是热销产品。
7. 供你方参考，花生价格已经调整到伦敦到岸价每公吨人们币5,000元。
8. 按照你方3月10日来信要求，现报1,000台新科DVD机如下。
9. 为了展开双方具体的业务，我们很高兴就2,500台海信计算机的向你方发盘如下，以我方最后确认为准。
10. 如果你们将报价降低2%，你们的产品便具有足够的竞争力了。

IV. Translate the following sentences into Chinese:
1. We can safely say that our prices are quite realistic; it's impossible that any other suppliers can make lower quotation if their goods are as good as ours in quality.

2. We appreciate the good quality of your products, but unfortunately your prices appear to be on the high side. We regret that at these prices we cannot place an order.

3. As business has been done extensively in your market at this price, we regret that we can not accept your counter-offer. It is our hope that you would reconsider the matter and let us know your decision as soon as possible.

4. All quotations are subject to our final confirmation. Unless otherwise stated or agreed upon, all prices are net without commission.

5. Only 0.5% is to be deducted from the CIF price, if buyers like to trade with us on CFR basis and insure the goods themselves.

6. We feel sure that a fair comparison of the quality between our products and similar articles from other sources will convince you of the reasonableness of our quotations.

7. We are prepared to keep our offer open until the end of this month and, as this product is now in great demand and the supply rather limited, we would recommend you to accept this offer as soon as possible.

8. We assure you that any further enquiries from you will receive our prompt attention.

9. Had you contacted us earlier, we could have complied with your request to the full.

10. But now, with our stock appreciably diminished, the maximum we can supply is 50 tons. The remainder can be replaced by 10 tons of Zinc Oxide 99%, which is a new type but priced lower by 5%. Of course, this substitution is subject to your approval.

V. Letter writing:

Write a firm offer which should cover the following details:

1. 产品：铜；
2. 可提供60公吨铜；
3. 价格低廉：成本加运费到上海价每吨800美元；
4. 订货一个月内交货；
5. 货款以我方为收益人的不可撤销的信用证，凭即期汇票在伦敦以英镑支付；
6. 以上实盘，本月底前报到我方有效。

Chapter Five

Conclusion of Business

Part I Introduction

Business is concluded when the seller and buyer sign a sales contract or sales confirmation after the seller accepts and confirms the buyer's order based on what they have negotiated. Differences in terminology and language may bring about misunderstandings, not to mention the mistakes possibly made in typing and transmitting messages. Therefore, it is particularly important to sign a sales contract or a sales confirmation so as to ensure the performance of it based on their identical understanding of the terms and conditions agreed upon.

The contract or sales confirmation can be either formal or informal. The formal ones are very often preprinted in a certain pattern, which simplifies the procedures in those deals covering similar or same goods and similar or same terms and conditions. The receiver of the draft sales contract can advise to make amendments as he desires, if he finds terms and conditions unfair or unacceptable.

Either in a formal contract or sales confirmation, special attention should be paid to the terms of price, terms of payment, specifications, quality, time of delivery, port of destination, etc.

Part II Sample Letters

Sample 1 Garlic

Dear Sirs,

Re: 1,350 M/T Garlic 2012 Crop

We are confirming your order No. 276 for 1,350 metric tons of Garlic FAQ 2012 Crop at US$942 per m/t CIF Geneva for shipment during April/May.

As regards the terms of payment, we wish to reiterate that our customary practice is by 100% Confirmed, Irrevocable Transferable and Divisible Letter of Credit in our favor to be available by sight draft and remain valid for negotiation in China until the 10th day after the aforesaid time of shipment. As requested in your previous letter, we have sent

Chapter Five

you our Sales Confirmation No. 321 in duplicate, one copy of which please sign and return us for file.

We appreciate your faithful cooperation and hope that our handling this first order of yours will lead to further business between us.

We anticipate hearing from you soon.

Yours faithfully,

Notes
1. Geneva（瑞士）日内瓦
2. as regards 关于
   类似的短语还有：
   with regard to, regarding, as to, as for, in connection with, as concerns, concerning, with reference, referring to
   Regarding your counter-offer, we regret that we are not in a position to meet your requirement.
   关于你方的还盘，很抱歉我方不能满足你方的要求。
3. reiterate v. 重申，反复地说
   The government has reiterated that the rights and interests of people are of first priority.
   政府重申人民的权利和利益是首要的。
   The miners have reiterated their demand for an increase in their pay.
   矿工们重申要求加薪。
4. customary practice/ usual practice 习惯做法，惯例
   It's our usual practice to pack tea in wooden cases.
   我们的习惯做法是用木箱包装茶叶。
5. ... by 100% Confirmed, Irrevocable, Transferable and Divisible Letter of Credit in our favor to be available by sight draft and to remain valid for negotiation in China until the 10th day of the aforesaid time of shipment.
   开给我方100%保兑的、不撤消的、可转让的、可分割的即期付款信用证，并注明在上述装运日期后10天内在中国议付有效。
6. sight draft 即期汇票
7. negotiation n. 议付，即卖方按与银行商定的结汇方式凭单到银行结汇
   negotiation bank（信用证）议付行
8. in duplicate 一式两份
   in triplicate 一式三份
   in quadruplicate, in four copies 一式四份
   in five copies 一式五份
9. anticipate v. + v-ing /that 期望，预期
   We are not anticipating that there will be trouble when we start business.
   我们期望真正开始交易时没有什么麻烦。
10. return for file 回签存档
    Please sign and return one copy for our file soon.
    请尽快回签一份，以备我方存档。

Sample 2 Counter-signature

Dear Sirs,

We have duly received your Sales Contract No. 19 covering the software we have booked with you. Enclosed please find the duplicate with our counter-signature. Thanks to our mutual efforts, we are able to bridge the price gap and put the deal through.

The relative L/C has been established with the Bank of China, London, in your favor. It will reach you in due course.

Please follow the shipping instructions and make sure that our order is executed to the entire satisfaction of our customers and with the least possible delay.

Regarding further quantities required, we hope you will see your way clear to make us an offer. As an indication, we are prepared to order 5,000 pieces.

Yours faithfully,

Notes
1. bridge the gap 弥合差距
   It needs mutual efforts to bridge the price gap.
   弥合价格差距需要双方共同的努力。
2. put through 完成
   We believe that we can put through the business if you renew your offer for another week.
   我方相信如果你方能把报盘期限再宽限一周，双方定能达成贸易。
3. execute v. 执行
   Please do your utmost to execute this order, as it will lead to other business.
   请尽可能执行合同，因为它将带来其他更多的合同。
   We assure you that we can execute your order punctually.
   我们向您保证能准时执行你方的定单。
4. indication n. 概念，示意
   indication of price= idea of price 价格意见
   Please give us indication of the price at which you think you would close.
   请告知您认为能成交的价格意见。

Sample 3 Ladies' and Children's Shoes

Dear Sirs,

We thank you for your order of April 24, 2011 for Ladies' and Children shoes and confirm the supply of 2,000 pairs of shoes at the prices stated in your Order No. 56 with a special discount on your order worth or above US$ 6,000.

Our Sales Confirmation No.123 in two originals have been airmailed to you. Please sign and return one copy of them for our file.

It is understood that a letter of credit in our favor covering the said shoes should be opened immediately. We wish to point out that the stipulations in the relative L/C must strictly conform to those stated in our Sales Confirmation so as to avoid subsequent amendments. You may rest assured that we will effect shipment without delay on receipt of your letter of credit.

We appreciate your cooperation and look forward to receiving your further orders.

Yours faithfully,

Notes
1. original *n.* 正本 *adj.* 正本的，原先的
   These are original bills of lading.
   这些都是正本提单。
   We want two originals and three copies.
   我们要正本两份，副本三份。
   This contract is made out in two originals in both Chinese and English.
   本合同制成中英文正本两份。
2. amendment *n.* 修改，修改书
   The wording of the agreement calls for amendment.
   协议书的措辞需要修改。
   Please rush the amendment to the L/C.
   请对信用证速作修改。
   We enclose amendment advice of L/C No. 50.
   兹附寄第50号信用证的修改通知。
3. stipulation *n.* a condition in a contract or agreement 规定，条款
   ...the stipulations in the relative L/C must strictly conform to those stated in our Sales Confirmation
   相关信用证的规定必须严格符合售货确认书的规定。
4. subsequent *adj.* following 随后的
   ... so as to avoid subsequent amendments 以避免随后的修改
   Please make sure to carry out our order carefully so as to avoid subsequent troubles.
   请务必认真执行我方订单，以避免日后麻烦。

Sample 4 Canned Beef

Dear Sirs,

We are very pleased to confirm the agreement on your order No. 358 for Canned Beef as follows:
Description: A-I Grade Canned Beef of the following four specifications:

        A. 220 GM net weight
        B. 365 GM net weight
        C. 480 GM net weight
        D. 520 GM net weight

Packing: By standard export case of 100 cans each
Unit price: CIF net New York per case in US dollars
        A. 32
        B. 38
        C. 40
        D. 57

Payment: By 100% irrevocable letter of credit opened immediately through First National City Bank, N.Y., and drawn at sight.

Delivery: For item A and B: prompt shipment
        For item C and D: one month after receipt of L/C

Shipping Marks: As per our usual practice

Remark: In addition to the ordinary shipping documents, please also submit Certificate of Origin for each shipment.

We are attaching our Sales Confirmation No.45 in duplicate, one copy of which please countersign and return to us for our file. We trust you will open the relative L/C at an early date.

Hoping the goods will turn out to your entire satisfaction and we may have further orders from you.

Yours faithfully,

Notes
1. A-I Grade 甲级
   canned (Am. E.), tinned (Br. E.) 罐装的
   canned beans/fruits/fish/beef 罐装青豆/水果/鱼/牛肉
2. shipping marks 装运标志，唛头
   shipping advice/notice 装船通知（货物装船后发出）
   shipping instruction 装船指示
   shipping space 舱位
   shipping order 装货单，下货纸
   shipment *n.* 装船，船货
   goods awaiting shipment 待运货物
   port of shipment 装货港
   shipment ex m. Sun 太阳号轮船卸下的货
3. countersign *v.* 连署，会签
   counter signature 连署签名
   After the Sales Contract has been signed by the seller, it will be countersigned by the buyer.
   售货合同经卖方签署后，买方将会签。

Sample 5 Entrust an Exclusive Agency

Dear Sirs,

We have received your letter of 15th and are favorably impressed with the proposal you made. You are kindly informed that we have decided to entrust you with the exclusive agency for our TCL Trump High-definition Television Sets in the territory of Pakistan.

The exclusive agency agreement has been drawn up for duration of one year, automatically renewable on expiration for a similar period unless a written notice is given to the contrary. Enclosed please find a copy of the draft. It is highly appreciated if you could go over the provisions and advise us whether they meet with your approval.

We shall do our best to assist you in establishing a mutually beneficial trade.

Yours faithfully,

Notes

1. entrust *n.* 委托
   exclusive agency 独家代理
   exclusive agency agreement 独家代理协议
   You are kindly informed that we have decided to entrust you with the exclusive agency for our TCL Trump High-definition Television Sets in the territory of Pakistan.
   谨此通知贵方，我方已决定委托贵方作为我方TCL王牌高清晰电视机在巴基斯坦的独家代理。
2. renewable *adj.* (合同或协议)可延期的，可续签的
   A formal contract is signed which is renewable annually.
   正式签订了每年可续签的合同。
3. The exclusive agency agreement has been drawn up for duration of one year, automatically renewable on expiration for a similar period unless a written notice is given to the contrary.
   为期一年的独家代理协议已制定，期满自动续期一年，除非书面通知表示反对。
4. provision *n.* 规定，条款
   Any failure to enforce any provision of this Agreement shall not constitute a waiver thereof or of any other provision except as set forth herein.
   任何违法行为将不会因为此协议而免除责任，除非双方另有书面协议。

Sample 6 独家代理协议
Exclusive Agency Agreement

为发展业务关系，有关双方在平等互利基础上，于____年____月____日在____（地点）订立本协议，双方同意并约定如下：

This agreement is made and entered into by and between the parties concerned on _____ (Date) in _____ (Place) on the basis of equality and mutual benefit to develop business on terms and conditions mutually agreed upon as follows:

1. 协议双方
   The Parties Concerned
   甲方：_____   乙方：_____
   Party A: _____   Party B: _____
   地址：_____   地址：_____
   Add: _____   Add: _____
   电话：_____   电话：_____
   Tel: _____   Tel: _____
   传真：_____   传真：_____
   Fax: _____   Fax: _____

2. 委任
   Appointment
   甲方指定乙方为其独家代理，就第三条项下的商品从第四条规定的区域顾客中招揽订单，乙方接受上述委任。
   Party A hereby appoints Party B as its Exclusive Agent to solicit orders for the commodity stipulated in Article 3 from customers in the territory stipulated in Article 4, and Party B accepts and assumes such appointment.

3. 代理商品
   Commodity _____

4. 代理区域
   Territory
   仅限于_____（比如：中国）
   In the territory of _____ only. (For example, China)

5. 最低业务量
   Minimum Turnover
   乙方同意，在本协议有效期内从上述代理区域内招揽顾客购买上述商品，订单金额不低于_____美元。
   Party B shall undertake to solicit orders for the above commodity from customers in the above territory during the effective period of this agreement for not less than USD _____.

6. 价格与支付
   Price and Payment
   每一笔交易的货物价格应由乙方与买主通过谈判确定，并须经甲方最后确认。
   由买方开出以甲方为受益人的、保兑的、不可撤销的信用证付款。信用证须在装运日期前_____天到达甲方。
   The price for each individual transaction shall be fixed through negotiations between Party B and the buyer, and subject to Party A's final confirmation.
   Payment shall be made by confirmed, irrevocable L/C opened by the buyer in favor

of Party A, which shall reach Party A _____ days before the date of shipment.

7. 独家代理权
   Exclusive Right
   基于本协议授予的独家代理权，甲方不得直接或间接地通过乙方以外的渠道向中国顾客销售或出口第三条所列商品，乙方不得在中国经销、分销或促销与上述商品相竞争或类似的产品，也不得招揽或接受旨在中国以外地区销售为目的的订单，在本协议有效期内，甲方应将其收到的来自中国其他商家的有关代理产品的询价或订单转交给乙方。
   In consideration of the exclusive rights granted herein, Party A shall not, directly or indirectly, sell or export the commodity stipulated in Article 3 to customers in China through channels other than Party B; Party B shall not sell, distribute or promote the sales of any products competitive with or similar to the above commodity in China and shall not solicit or accept orders for the purpose of selling them outside China. Party A shall refer to Party B any enquiries or orders for the commodity in question received by Party A from other firms in China during the validity of this agreement.

8. 商情报告
   Market Report
   为使甲方充分了解现行市场情况，乙方至少每季度提供一次或在必要时随时向甲方提供市场报告，包括与本协议代理商品的进口与销售有关的地方法规的变动、当地市场发展趋势以及买方对甲方按协议供应的货物的品质、包装、价格等方面的意见。乙方还向甲方提供其他供应商类似商品的报价和广告资料。
   In order to keep Party A well informed of the prevailing market conditions, Party B should undertake to supply Party A, at least once a quarter or at any time when necessary, with market reports concerning changes of the local regulations in connection with the import and sales of the commodity covered by this agreement, local market tendency and the buyer's comments on quality, packing, price, etc. of the goods supplied by Party A under this agreement. Party B shall also supply Party A with quotations and advertising materials on similar products of other suppliers.

9. 广告及费用
   Advertising and Expenses
   乙方负担本协议有效期内在中国销售代理商品做广告宣传的一切费用，并向甲方提交用于广告的声像资料，供甲方事先核准。
   Party A shall bear all expenses for advertising and publicity in connection with the commodity in question in China within the validity of this agreement, and shall submit to Party A all audio and video materials intended for advertising for prior approval.

10. 佣金
    Commission
    对乙方直接获取并经甲方确认接受的订单，甲方按净发票售价向乙方支付_____%的佣金。佣金在甲方收到每笔订单的全部货款后_____天内向乙方支付。
    Party A shall pay Party B a commission of_____% on the net invoiced selling price on all orders directly obtained by Party B and accepted by party A. Within days from the date Party A receives the full payment for each order, Party A shall

pay the commission to Party B.

11. 政府部门间的交易
    Transactions Between Governmental Bodies
    在甲、乙双方政府部门之间达成的交易不受本协议条款的限制，此类交易的金额也不应计入第五条规定的最低业务量。
    Transactions concluded between governmental bodies of Party A and Party B shall not be restricted by the terms and conditions of this agreement, nor shall the amount of such transactions be counted as part of the turnover stipulated in Article 5.

12. 工业产权
    Industrial Property Rights
    在本协议有效期内，为销售有关 _____（代理商品），乙方可以使用甲方拥有的商标，并承认使用于或包含于 _____（代理商品）中的任何专利商标、版权或其他工业产权为甲方独家拥有。一旦发现侵权，乙方应立即通知甲方并协助甲方采取措施，保护甲方权益。
    Party B may use the trade-marks owned by Party A for the sale of _____ (commodity) covered herein within the validity of this agreement, and shall acknowledge that all patents, trademarks, copy rights or any other industrial property rights used or embodied in _____ (commodity) shall remain to be the sole properties of Party A. Should any infringement be found, Party B shall promptly notify and assist Party A to take steps to protect the latter's rights.

13. 协议有效期
    Validity of Agreement
    本协议经有关双方如期签署后生效，有效期为_____年，从_____年_____月_____日至_____年_____月_____日。除非有内容相反通知，本协议期满后将延长_____个月。
    This agreement, when duly signed by the both parties concerned, shall remain effect for _____ months from _____ (date) to _____ (date), and it shall be extended for another _____ months upon expiration unless notice in writing is given to the contrary.

14. 协议的终止
    Termination
    在本协议有效期内，如果发现一方违背协议条款，另一方有权终止协议。
    During the validity of this agreement, if either of the two parties is found to have violated the stipulations herein, the other party has the right to terminate this agreement.

15. 不可抗力
    Force Majeure
    由于水灾、火灾、地震、干旱、战争或协议一方无法预见、控制、避免和克服的其他事件导致不能或暂时不能全部或部分履行本协议，该方不负责任。但是，受不可抗力事件影响的一方须尽快将发生的事件通知另一方，并在不可抗力事件发生15天内将有关机构出具的不可抗力事件的证明寄交对方。
    Either party shall not be held responsible for failure or delay to perform all or any part of this agreement due to flood, fire, earthquake, draught, war or any other

events which could not be predicted, controlled, avoided or overcome by the relative party. However, the party affected by the event of Force Majeure shall inform the other party of its occurrence in writing as soon as possible and thereafter send a certificate of the event issued by the relevant authorities to the other party within 15 days after its occurrence.

16. 仲裁

    Arbitration

    因履行本协议所发生的一切争议应通过友好协商解决，如协商不能解决争议，则应提交中国国际经济贸易仲裁委员会华南分会，按照申请仲裁时该会实施的仲裁规则进行仲裁。仲裁裁决是终局的，对双方均有约束力。

    Any dispute arising from the performance of this agreement shall be settled through friendly negotiation. Should no settlement be reached through negotiation, the case shall then be submitted to China International Economic and Trade Arbitration Commission, South China Sub-Commission for arbitration, which shall be conducted in accordance with the Commission's arbitration rules in effect at the time of applying for arbitration. The arbitral award is final and binding upon both parties.

    甲方：_____　　　　　　　乙方：_____
    　　（签字）　　　　　　　　　　　　　（签字）
    　　Party A：_____　　　　　party B：_____
    　　（Signature）　　　　　　　　　　　（Signature）

Part III　Reading Materials

1. INCOTERMS 2010

There are totally 11 price terms which divide the costs and liabilities between the buyers and the sellers. They are put into 4 groups. Some terms are only applicable to marine transportation while others are applicable to all modes of transportation.

Group E Term

EXW [1] (named place of delivery) —EX Works

This is the only term in this group. This rule may be used irrespective of the mode of transport selected and may also be used where more than one mode of transport is employed. It is suitable for domestic trade, while FCA is usually more appropriate for international trade.

"Ex Works" means that the seller delivers when it places the goods at the disposal of the buyer at the seller's premises or at another named place (i.e., works, factory, warehouse, etc.). The seller does not need to load the goods on any collecting vehicle, nor does it need to clear the goods for export, where such clearance is applicable.

The parties are well advised to specify as clearly as possible the point within the named place of delivery, as the costs and risks to that point are for the account of the seller. The buyer bears all costs and risks involved in taking the goods from the agreed point, if any, at the named place of delivery.

Group F Terms

F terms refer to FAS, FCA, FOB. FAS is the short term of "Free Alongside Ship," and FCA is the short form of "Free Carrier" while FOB is the short form of "Free on Board."

FAS[②] (named port of shipment) —Free Alongside Ship

This rule is to be used only for sea or inland waterway transport. "Free Alongside Ship" means that the seller delivers when the goods are placed alongside the vessel (e.g., on a quay or a barge) nominated by the buyer at the named port of shipment. The risk of loss of or damage to the goods passes when the goods are alongside the ship, and the buyer bears all costs from that moment onwards. The parties are well advised to specify as clearly as possible the loading point at the named port of shipment, as the costs and risks to that point are for the account of the seller and these costs and associated handling charges may vary according to the practice of the port. The seller is required either to deliver the goods alongside the ship or to procure goods already so delivered for shipment. The reference to "procure" here caters for multiple sales down a chain ("string sales"), particularly common in the commodity trades.

Where the goods are in containers, it is typical for the seller to hand the goods over to the carrier at a terminal and not alongside the vessel. In such situations, the FAS rule would be inappropriate, and the FCA rule should be used. FAS requires the seller to clear the goods for export, where applicable. However, the seller has no obligation to clear the goods for import, pay any import duty or carry out any import customs formalities.

FCA[③] (named place of delivery) —Free Carrier

This rule may be used irrespective of the mode of transport selected and may also be used where more than one mode of transport is employed. "Free Carrier" means that the seller delivers the goods to the carrier or another person nominated by the buyer at the seller's premises or another named place. The parties are well advised to specify as clearly as possible the point within the named place of delivery, as the risk passes to the buyer at that point. If the parties intend to deliver the goods at the seller's premises, they should identify the address of those premises as the named place of delivery. If, on the other hand, the parties intend the goods to be delivered at another place, they must identify a different specific place of delivery.

FCA requires the seller to clear the goods for export, where applicable. However, the seller has no obligation to clear the goods for import, pay any import duty or carry out any import customs formalities.

FOB[④] (named port of shipment) —Free on Board

This rule is to be used only for sea or inland waterway transport. "Free on Board" means that the seller delivers the goods on board the vessel nominated by the buyer at the named port of shipment or procures the goods already so delivered. The risk of loss of or damage to the goods passes when the goods are on board the vessel, and the buyer bears all costs from that moment onwards.

The seller is required either to deliver the goods on board the vessel or to procure goods already so delivered for shipment. The reference to "procure" here caters for multiple sales down a chain ("string sales"), particularly common in the commodity trades.

FOB may not be appropriate where goods are handed over to the carrier before they are on board the vessel, for example goods in containers, which are typically delivered at a terminal. In such situations, the FCA rule should be used.

FOB requires the seller to clear the goods for export, where applicable. However, the seller has no obligation to clear the goods for import, pay any import duty or carry out any import customs formalities.

Group C Terms

C Terms refer to CFR, CIF, CPT, and CIP. Under this group, the seller will cover the cost arising from the main carriage.

CFR[5] (named port of destination) —Cost and Freight

This rule is to be used only for sea or inland waterway transport. "Cost and Freight" means that the seller delivers the goods on board the vessel or procures the goods already so delivered. The risk of loss of or damage to the goods passes when the goods are on board the vessel.

The seller must contract for and pay the costs and freight necessary to bring the goods to the named port of destination. When CPT, CIP, CFR or CIF are used, the seller fulfils its obligation to deliver when it hands the goods over to the carrier in the manner specified in the chosen rule and not when the goods reach the place of destination.

This rule has two critical points, because risk passes and costs are transferred at different places. While the contract will always specify a destination port, it might not specify the port of shipment, which is where risk passes to the buyer. If the shipment port is of particular interest to the buyer, the parties are well advised to identify it as precisely as possible in the contract.

The parties are well advised to identify as precisely as possible the point at the agreed port of destination, as the costs to that point are for the account of the seller. The seller is advised to procure contracts of carriage that match this choice precisely. If the seller incurs costs under its contract of carriage related to unloading at the specified point at the port of destination, the seller is not entitled to recover such costs from the buyer unless otherwise agreed between the parties.

The seller is required either to deliver the goods on board the vessel or to procure goods already so delivered for shipment to the destination.

In addition, the seller is required either to make a contract of carriage or to procure such a contract. The reference to "procure" here caters for multiple sales down a chain ("string sales"), particularly common in the commodity trades.

CIF[6] (named port of destination) —Cost, Insurance, and Freight

This rule is to be used only for sea or inland waterway transport. "Cost, Insurance and Freight" means that the seller delivers the goods on board the vessel or procures the goods already so delivered. The risk of loss of or of damage to the goods passes when the goods are on board the vessel. The seller must contract for and pay the costs and freight necessary to bring the goods to the named port of destination.

The seller also contracts for insurance cover against the buyer's risk of loss of or damage to the goods during the carriage. The buyer should note that under CIF the seller is required to obtain insurance only on minimum cover. Should the buyer wish to have more insurance protection, it will need either to agree as much expressly with the seller or to make its own extra insurance arrangements.

This rule has two critical points, because risk passes and costs are transferred at different places. While the contract will always specify a destination port, it might not specify the port of shipment, which is where risk passes to the buyer. If the shipment port is of particular interest to the buyer, the parties are well advised to identify it as precisely as possible in the contract.

The parties are well advised to identify as precisely as possible the point at the agreed port of destination, as the costs to that point are for the account of the seller. The seller is advised to procure contracts of carriage that match this choice precisely. If the seller incurs costs under its contract of carriage related to unloading at the specified point at the port of destination, the seller is not entitled to recover such costs from the buyer unless otherwise agreed between the parties.

The seller is required either to deliver the goods on board the vessel or to procure goods already so delivered for shipment to the destination. In addition the seller is required either to make a contract of carriage or to procure such a contract. The reference to "procure" here caters for multiple sales down a chain ('string sales'), particularly common in the commodity trades.

CIF may not be appropriate where goods are handed over to the carrier before they are on board the vessel, for example goods in containers, which are typically delivered at a terminal. In such circumstances, the CIP rule should be used. CIF requires the seller to clear the goods for export, where applicable. However, the seller has no obligation to clear the goods for import, pay any import duty or carry out any import customs formalities.

CPT[7] (named place of destination)—Carriage Paid to

This rule may be used irrespective of the mode of transport selected and may also be used where more than one mode of transport is employed. "Carriage Paid to" means that the seller delivers the goods to the carrier or another person nominated by the seller at an agreed place (if any such place is agreed between the parties) and that the seller must contract for and pay the costs of carriage necessary to bring the goods to the named place of destination.

When CPT, CIP, CFR or CIF are used, the seller fulfils its obligation to deliver when it hands the goods over to the carrier and not when the goods reach the place of destination.

This rule has two critical points, because risk passes and costs are transferred at different places. The parties are well advised to identify as precisely as possible in the contract both the place of delivery, where the risk passes to the buyer, and the named place of destination to which the seller must contract for the carriage. If several carriers are used for the carriage to the agreed destination and the parties do not agree on a specific point of delivery, the default position is that risk passes when the goods have been delivered to the first carrier at a point entirely of the seller's choosing and over which the buyer has no control. Should the parties wish the risk to pass at a later stage (e.g., at an ocean port or airport), they need to specify this in their contract of sale. The parties are also well advised to identify as precisely as possible the point within the agreed place of destination, as the costs to that point are for the account of the seller. The seller is advised to procure contracts of carriage that match this choice precisely. If the seller incurs costs under its contract of carriage related to unloading at the named place of destination, the seller is not entitled to recover such costs from the buyer unless otherwise agreed between the parties.

CPT requires the seller to clear the goods for export, where applicable. However, the seller has no obligation to clear the goods for import, pay any import duty or carry out any import customs formalities.

CIP® (named place of destination) — Carriage and Insurance Paid to

This rule may be used irrespective of the mode of transport selected and may also be used where more than one mode of transport is employed. "Carriage and Insurance Paid to" means that the seller delivers the goods to the carrier or another person nominated by the seller at an agreed place (if any such place is agreed between the parties) and that the seller must contract for and pay the costs of carriage necessary to bring the goods to the named place of destination.

The seller also contracts for insurance cover against the buyer's risk of loss of or damage to the goods during the carriage. The buyer should note that under CIP the seller is required to obtain insurance only on minimum cover. Should the buyer wish to have more insurance protection, it will need either to agree as much expressly with the seller or to make its own extra insurance arrangements.

This rule has two critical points, because risk passes and costs are transferred at different places. The parties are well advised to identify as precisely as possible in the contract both the place of delivery, where the risk passes to the buyer, and the named place of destination to which the seller must contract for carriage. If several carriers are used for the carriage to the agreed destination and the parties do not agree on a specific point of delivery, the default position is that risk passes when the goods have been delivered to the first carrier at a point entirely of the seller's choosing and over which the buyer has no control. Should the parties wish the risk to pass at a later stage (e.g., at an ocean port or an airport), they need to specify this in their contract of sale.

The parties are also well advised to identify as precisely as possible the point within the agreed place of destination, as the costs to that point are for the account of the seller. The seller is advised to procure contracts of carriage that match this choice precisely. If the seller incurs costs under its contract of carriage related to unloading at the named place of destination, the seller is not entitled to recover such costs from the buyer unless otherwise agreed between the parties.

CIP requires the seller to clear the goods for export, where applicable. However, the seller has no obligation to clear the goods for import, pay any import duty or carry out any import customs formalities.

Group D Terms

There are three D terms: DAT, DAP, and DDP. Group D is different from Group C in that, under D terms, the seller is responsible for the arrival of the goods at the agreed place or point of destination. The seller must bear all the risks and costs in bringing the cargoes thereto. Hence, contracts under D terms mean arrival contracts while contracts under C Terms mean shipment contracts.

DAT[9] (named terminal at port or place of destination) — Delivered at Terminal

This rule, as the new-added part, may be used irrespective of the mode of transport selected and may also be used where more than one mode of transport is employed. "Delivered at Terminal" means that the seller delivers when the goods, once unloaded from the arriving means of transport, are placed at the disposal of the buyer at a named terminal at the named port or place of destination. "Terminal" includes any place, whether covered or not, such as a quay, warehouse, container yard or road, rail or air cargo terminal.

The seller bears all risks involved in bringing the goods to and unloading them at the terminal at the named port or place of destination. The parties are well advised to specify as clearly as possible the terminal and, if possible, a specific point within the terminal at the agreed port or place of destination, as the risks to that point are for the account of the seller. The seller is advised to procure a contract of carriage that matches this choice precisely.

Moreover, if the parties intend the seller to bear the risks and costs involved in transporting and handling the goods from the terminal to another place, then the DAP or DDP rules should be used.

DAT requires the seller to clear the goods for export, where applicable. However, the seller has no obligation to clear the goods for import, pay any import duty or carry out any import customs formalities.

DAP[10] (named place of destination) — Delivered at Place

This rule, another new-added part, may be used irrespective of the mode of transport selected and may also be used where more than one mode of transport is employed. "Delivered at Place" means that the seller delivers when the goods are placed at the disposal of the buyer on the arriving means of transport ready for unloading at the named place of destination. The seller bears all risks involved in bringing the goods to the named place.

The parties are well advised to specify as clearly as possible the point within the agreed place of destination, as the risks to that point are for the account of the seller. The seller is advised to procure contracts of carriage that match this choice precisely. If the seller incurs costs under its contract of carriage related to unloading at the place of destination, the seller is not entitled to recover such costs from the buyer unless otherwise agreed between the parties.

DAP requires the seller to clear the goods for export, where applicable.

However, the seller has no obligation to clear the goods for import, pay any import duty or carry out any import customs formalities. If the parties wish the seller to clear the goods for import, pay any import duty and carry out any import customs formalities, the DDP term should be used.

DDP[11] (named place of destination) — Delivered Duty Paid

This rule may be used irrespective of the mode of transport selected and may also be used where more than one mode of transport is employed. "Delivered Duty Paid" means that the seller delivers the goods when the goods are placed at the disposal of the buyer, cleared for import on the arriving means of transport ready for unloading at the named place of destination. The seller bears all the costs and risks involved in bringing the goods to the place of destination and has an obligation to clear the goods not only for export but also for import, to pay any duty for both export and import and to carry out all customs formalities.

DDP represents the maximum obligation for the seller. The parties are well advised to specify as clearly as possible the point within the agreed place of destination, as the costs and risks to that point are for the account of the seller. The seller is advised to procure contracts of carriage that match this choice precisely. If the seller incurs costs under its contract of carriage related to unloading at the place of destination, the seller is not entitled to recover such costs from the buyer unless otherwise agreed between the parties.

The parties are well advised not to use DDP if the seller is unable directly or indirectly to obtain import clearance. If the parties wish the buyer to bear all risks and costs of import clearance, the DAP rule should be used.

Any VAT or other taxes payable upon import are for the seller's account unless expressly agreed otherwise in the sales contract.

Notes

① EXW (named place of delivery) 工厂交货（……指定交货地）
② FAS (named port of shipment) 装运港船边交货
③ FCA (named place of delivery) 货交承运人（……货交交货地）
④ FOB(named port of shipment) 装运港船上交货
⑤ CFR (named port of destination) 成本加运费
⑥ CIF (named port of destination) 成本、保险费加运费
⑦ CPT (named place of destination) 运费付至目的地
⑧ CIP (named place of destination) 运保费付至目的地
⑨ DAT(named place of destination) 运输终端交货
⑩ DAP(named place of destination) 目的地交货
⑪ DDP (named place of destination) 目的地完税价格

Questions

1. What are the main differences in liabilities and obligations between Group C and Group D?
2. Under which terms shall the buyer clear the goods for export? And under which terms is the seller to effect insurance?

2. Cross-Culture Negotiation

Some people argued that relating negotiation to communication skills and cultural knowledge is essential. However, negotiation is not just a single skill or even a group of skills. In the broad sense①, negotiation is a process that takes place in a particular context. The context, in terms of subject matter, the mature of the parties involved and the degree of formality②, determines the particular skills required in any specific negotiation situation. Some of these skills are common to all forms of negotiation while others are specific to a particular context.

In a mono-cultural environment③, the negotiation process is more predictable and accurate, as the negotiators do not have to be concerned with challenges of language or cultural differences. Behavior negotiation is consistent within cultures and each culture has its own distinctive④ negotiation style. Furthermore, as an individual's conduct during a negotiation is influenced by ethnic heritage and culturally embedded⑤ attitudes and customs individuals having the same cultural backgrounds tend to display common patterns of thinking, feeling and reacting in line with their cultural heritage. There are many more challenges in a cross-cultural environment than in a mono-cultural setting. Cross-cultural negotiations are negotiations where the negotiating parties belong to different cultures and do not share the same ways of thinking, feeling and behaving. The negotiation process is generally more complex because it encompasses unconscious forces of the different cultural norms that may undermine effective communication. In the negotiation process, interpersonal communication is the key activity that takes place at the verbal, nonverbal, situational, contextual level, and a total communication system can assist the negotiator bridge the gap between utterance⑥ and felt meaning. Thus, in a cross-cultural negotiation, in addition to the basic negotiation skills, it is important to understand the cultural differences, and to modify the negotiation style accordingly.

Notes

① broad sense 广义
② formality *n.* 手续；拘泥形式
③ mono-cultural environment 单一文化环境
④ distinctive *adj.* 明显区别的
⑤ embed *v.* 插入；牢记
⑥ utterance *n.* 发音，语调

> 国际商务谈判是商务活动重要的环节。由于谈判双方或多方来自不同的文化背景，不同的思维、感觉及行为使谈判成功与否具有很多不确定因素，因此商务谈判前要有文化准备；谈判中要考虑到文化因素，从而灵活、正确地应付谈判对手。

Questions

1. What determines the particular skills required in negotiations?
2. What factors make a successful cross-culture negotiation?

Chapter Five

Exercises

I. Fill in the blanks with the best choice:

1. Payment should be made _____ sight draft.
   a. at   b. upon   c. with   d. by
2. Mr. Smith could agree _____ D/P terms.
   a. with   b. to   c. in   d. over
3. You didn't say whether you wish the transaction to be _____ cash or _____ credit.
   a. in...on   b. at...on   c. on...on   d. by...by
4. We enclose a check for US$2,000 _____ payment of all commission due to you up to date.
   a. at   b. in   c. for   d. by
5. We make purchases _____ our own account.
   a. on   b. for   c. at   d. with
6. We will draw _____ you by our documentary draft at sight on collection basis.
   a. at   b. up   c. on   d. for
7. Contracts must be renewed one week _____ their expiration.
   a. on   b. against   c. the moment of   d. before
8. We thank you for your letter of May 5, _____ your purchase from us of 500 tons of Green Beans.
   a. confirm   b. to confirm   c. confirming   d. confirmed
9. We regret to report that a consignment of silk piece goods _____ Order No. 2 has not been delivered.
   a. with   b. under   c. at   d. on
10. As agreed upon in our negotiations, payment _____ L/C.
    a. by   b. will   c. is by   d. is to be made by

II. Fill in the blanks with proper words and expressions:

1. We rely on you to _____ this order to the entire satisfaction _____ our customers and _____ the least possible delay.
2. We hope to come _____ terms with you _____ this order.
3. We regret our inability to comply _____ your request _____ the shipping goods in early December.
4. Our offer is firm _____ five days and we expect to hear from you _____ the end of this month.
5. We are well experienced _____ this line and can place orders with you _____ large quantities if your prices are attractive enough.
6. We wish to invite your attention _____ the fact that the shipped goods are badly damaged _____ their arrival.
7. The relative L/C has been established _____ the Bank of China, Paris, _____ your favor.
8. We hope that, by our joint efforts, the business between us will be promoted to our mutual _____.
9. We wish to call your attention _____ the validity _____ the L/C, since there's

no possibility _____ L/C extension.
10. Please supply the goods in strict _____ with the particulars given, any deviation from _____ will be at your own risks, unless agreed and authorized by us.

III. Fill in the contract in English with the given particulars from the following letters:

Letters concerned:

(1) Enquiry

Copenhagen, July 25, 2012

Cathay Export Corporation
Beijing
China

Dear Sirs,

One of our clients in Odense is in the market for a parcel of 3,000 dozen Ladies' Pajamas. We would therefore ask you to make us an offer based on CIF Odense including our commission of 2%.

We shall appreciate it if you will arrange for shipment to be made as early as possible by direct steamer for Odense.

As usual, our sight irrevocable L/C will be opened in your favour 30 days before the time of shipment.

Yours faithfully,
COPENHAGEN TRADING CO. LTD.

(2) Offer

Beijing, August 2, 2012

Copenhagen Trading Co. Ltd.
Copenhagen
Denmark

Dear Sirs,

Thank you for your letter of July 25 inquiring for 3,000 dozen Ladies' Pajamas. We take pleasure in making you an offer as follows, subject to your acceptance reaching here not later than August 18:

3,000 dozen Art. No. 208 Ladies' Pajamas in pink, blue and yellow colors, equally assorted, with the size assortment of S/3, M/6, and L/3 per dozen, packed in cartons, at GBP26.00 per dozen CIFC2% Odense, for shipment from any Chinese port in October.

Please note that since there is no direct steamer available for Odense in October, we find it only possible to ship the parcel with transshipment at Copenhagen.

We look forward to your early reply.

Yours faithfully,
CATHAY EXPORT CORPORATION

(3) Acceptance

Copenhagen, August 9, 2012

Cathay Export Corporation,
Beijing, China

Dear Sirs,

Thank you for your letter of August 2 offering us 3,000 dozen Ladies' Pajamas at GBP26.00 per dozen CIFC2% Odense.

We are glad to have been able to prevail upon our client to accept your price, though they found it a bit on the high side.

We are now arranging with our bank for the relevant L/C. When making shipment, please kindly see to it that insurance is to be effected against All Risks and War Risk as per the China Insurance Clauses of 1st January, 1981, for 110% of the invoice value. As to the shipment mark, we will let you know soon.

Enclosed is our S/C No.5674 signed in Beijing on August 12, 2012. Please countersign and return one copy to us for file.

We are looking forward to your early reply.

Yours faithfully,
COPENHAGEN TRADING CO. LTD.

CONTRACT

No. 04 –115

Sellers:
Buyers:

This Contract is made by and between the Buyers and the Sellers, whereby the Buyers agree to buy and the Sellers agree to sell the under-mentioned commodity according to the terms and conditions stipulated below:

Commodity:
Specifications:
Quantity:
Unit Price:
Total Value:
Packing:
Shipping Mark:
Insurance:
Time of Shipment:
Port of Shipment:
Port of Destination:
Terms of Payment:
Done and signed in _____ on this _____ day and of _____.

IV. Translate the following sentences into English:

1. 兹决定按照你方4月30日寄来的报价及具体条件,向你方购买铁矿石5,000吨,希望在7月30前交货。
2. 我们很高兴能供一级货核桃仁,10/11月份船期。
3. 我们正在认真考虑你方的条件。有些条款暂时不能接受,但我们将对此事做进一步考虑,然后再与你沟通。
4. 我们决定委托你作为我方汽车在新加坡的独家代理。
5. 我们今天已由伦敦中国银行开立以你方为抬头的信用证计50,000英镑。
6. 由于你方定单数量较大,我们目前不能满足此需求,但是我们将尽最大努力为你方获取货源,一旦情况好转,一定告知。
7. 鉴于双方长期友好关系,我们破例接受D/P60天付款。
8. 在你方承兑我方金额58,000美元的见票3个月付款的汇票之后,你处米兰银行就会把装船单据交予你们。
9. 现随附我方售货合同第189号一式二份,请查收。如审查无误,请会签后退回一份存档。
10. 经过我们再三努力磋商,厂方答应接受订货,从明年1月起每月交100台。

V. Translate the following letter into English:

敬启者:

你方9月10日关于薯片的回盘已收到,现确认接受回盘如下:500吨薯片每吨成本加运费利物浦价240美元,包括5%佣金。质量符合样品Sp-03号,水分最高16%,装运期2011年11/12月份。

本品为散装,其数量及金额允许有5%增减,请贵方在开信用证时予以注意。我们希望在装运前一个月收到你方开立的保兑的、不可撤消的即期信用证,以便我方如期装运。至于保险,我方将按惯例根据中国人民保险公司现行保险条例,按发票金额的110%投保一切险和战争险。

VI. Letter writing:

Write a letter to conclude business which should cover the following details:

1. Confirm accepting your offer No. 20 for 60 metric tons of Green Peas FAQ 2011 Crop at US$ 23 per m/t CIF Rotterdam;
2. Other terms as per Purchase Confirmation No. 21;
3. Sign and return one copy for our file;
4. Follow our instructions and effect shipment as contracted;
5. We will open the relative L/C.

Chapter Six

Payment

Part I Introduction

In international trade practice, the buyer holds himself responsible for the payment to the seller of the agreed amount, in the agreed currency, within the agreed period of time and by the agreed method of payment.

1. Instruments

The ideal means of payment for any exporter in international trade is cash payment. In practice, however, sellers of goods never insist on their rights to demand cash for payment as it is considered not convenient. In cash payment, the risk is also not well-balanced between the seller and the buyer.

Instead of cash, instruments or bills are used in international trade. They include draft, promissory note and check. All of them are used for the payment or transfer of money, among which the most often used is draft.

(1) Bill of Exchange or Draft

A bill of exchange, also called draft, is defined as an unconditional order in writing addressed by one person to another, signed by the person giving it, requiring the person to whom it is addressed to pay on demand, or at a fixed or determinable future time, a certain sum of money, to, or to the order of a specified person, or to the bearer.

The following are three specimens of bill of exchange:

Specimen 1

No. 3768
CAD 14,000   Toronto, May 15, 2012
   On demand pay to Kevin Vardar or bearer the sum of CANADIAN DOLLAR FOURTEEN THOUSAND ONLY.

                                                                            (signed) Michael Damon

To: Mr. Paul Redford
     Vancouver

Specimen 2

	Dated	2000-6-3, GUANGZHOU, CHINA

No. <u>86153F4051</u>

Exchange for USD30, 000

At <u>60 days after date of shipment</u> sight of this First of Exchange (Second of the same tenor and date unpaid), pay to the Order of

<u>BANK OF CHINA GUANGZHOU BRANCH</u> the sum of

SAY U.S. DOLLARS USD THIRTY THOUSAND SENT ONLY

Drawn under <u>HUANGPU (CHINA)</u>

<u>L/C NO: WS061110</u>

<u>Dated: June 01, 2002</u>

TO HAROLD IMPORT COMPANY, INC 3150 C Street, Suite 101 -- Anchorage, Alaska 99503

TEL: 86-20-8345-6288 FAX: 86-2--8345-6289

GUANGDONG CEREALS & OILS
IMPORT & EXPORT CORPORATION
5F-10F Guitian Building Road, South, Guandong, China

Specimen 3

Drawn under ***DESUN GLOBAL BANK***   Irrevocable L/C No. ***RL04002***

Dated ***April 19, 2012***   Payable with interest ***4.5%*** per annum

No. ***RC0419I01***   EXCHANGE for ***USD 8,937.6***   China Beijing ***April 20, 2012***

At 60 days sight of this FIRST of Exchange (Second of Exchange being unpaid) pay to the order of ***NANJING DESUN TRADING CO., LTD*** the sum of ***U.S. DOLLAR EIGHT THOUSAND NINE HUNDRED THIRTY SEVEN AND CENTS SIXTY.***

To: ***DESUN GLOBAL BANK***

Nanjing Desun Trading Co., Ltd.

A bill of exchange involves three parties: the drawer, the drawee (or the payer) and the payee.

The drawer is the person who draws or issues the bill of exchange and gives directions to the person to make a specific payment of money.

The drawee is the person to whom the order is addressed and who is to pay a certain sum of money to the payee upon the presentation of the bill.

The payee is the creditor of the bill, or in other words, the person to whom the payment is ordered to be made. The drawer and payee may be often the same person.

(2) Promissory Note

A promissory note is an unconditional promise in writing made by one person to another signed by the maker, engaging to pay, on demand or at a fixed or determinable future time, a certain sum of money to, or to the order of, a specified person or to the bearer.

Chapter Six

The main difference between a promissory note and a bill of exchange is that there are only two parties involved in the former, namely the maker (instead of drawer) and the payee. The maker undertakes to pay to the payee. While in the latter, three parties are involved. They are the drawer, drawee and the payee.

The following is the specimen of Promissory Note:

```
                        Promissory Note

    Singapore, 31.01.2000        Amount   US$ 250,000

    On  25 April 2000    we promise to pay against this Promissory Note
    the sum of  US Dollars Two hundred and fifty thousand
    to the order of  UK Export Company Ltd
    for value  Received

    Payable at:                  For and on behalf of:
    UK Export Banking Company plc   Import Buyer Company
    Sterling Street              Singapore
    London, UK
                                       C.E. Lee
                                 Managing Director
```

(3) Check

A check is an unconditional order in writing drawn on a banker signed by the drawer, requiring the banker to pay on demand a certain sum of money to, or to the order of a specified person or to the bearer. Checks are chiefly used in domestic trade.

2. Payment Methods

Basically, the methods of payment include remittance, collection and letter of credit. To choose a method for the payment of the goods, one needs to consider some factors such as credit, bank charges and formalities, etc.

(1) Remittance

Under remittance, the buyer delivers the payment of the goods to the seller by bank transfer. Four parties are involved in remittance: the remitter, the beneficiary (payee), the remitting bank, and the paying bank.

In international trade, remittance is often adopted in sales under the terms of payment in advance, cash with order, delivery first and payment afterwards for small quantity of goods or for payment of commission and sundry charges.

There are three types of remittance: Mail Transfer (M/T), Telegraphic Transfer (T/T) and Demand Draft (D/D). Mail Transfer is the most common method of remittance, by which the buyer hands over the payment of the goods to the remitting bank (his local bank) that, then, issues a trust deed for payment and sends it to the paying bank (its branch or correspondent bank) in the country of the beneficiary by mail authorizing payment to the seller. Mail Transfer costs less but is slower.

Telegraphic Transfer is similar to Mail Transfer except that the authorization of payment from the remitting bank to the paying bank is made by telegraphic means. Telegraphic Transfer is more expensive but takes much less time.

Under Demand Draft, the remitting bank, at the request of the buyer, draws a demand draft on its branch or correspondent bank instructing it to make payment to the seller on behalf of the buyer.

(2) Collection

Under collection, the exporter draws a bill of exchange on the importer for the sum due, with or without shipping documents attached, and then forwarded them to the bank in his place (the remitting bank), authorizing his bank to effect the collection of the payment of goods through its branch bank or correspondent bank in the importer's country.

Collection can be documentary collection, which has the relevant shipping documents attached to the bill of exchange, or clean collection, which uses only bills of exchange. Documentary collection is more often used in the payment of goods in international trade while clean collection is occasionally used in the payment of payment balance, extra charges and so on.

Four parties are involved in collection: Principal (usually the seller of the goods), the Remitting Bank (usually the bank in the seller's country), Collecting Bank (usually the bank in the buyer's country) and Drawee (usually the buyer of the goods).

Documentary collection falls into two varieties: documents against payment (D/P) and documents against acceptance (D/A). Under D/P, the collecting bank with instructions will not release the documents to the buyer until the full amount of payment is effected, while under D/A, the buyer can get the documents from the collecting bank after he has duly accepted the draft.

(3) Letter of Credit

In brief, a letter of credit (L/C) is a document addressed to the seller, written and signed by a bank, upon the request of the buyer. The bank, in issuing the L/C, promises to effect the payment of the goods to the seller if the seller conforms exactly to the conditions set forth in the letter of credit. Letter of Credit is now the most often used method of payment in international trade.

Parties involved in L/C are:

The applicant (usually the buyer), the opening or issuing bank (usually in the buyer's country, which opens the L/C upon the request of the buyer), the advising or notifying bank (usually in the seller's country, which advises the seller of the establishment of L/C), the beneficiary (usually the seller), the negotiating bank (the bank that pays or accepts the draft presented by the seller), the paying bank (usually the issuing bank, which is designated by the L/C to pay the draft), and confirming bank (usually the bank asked by the opening bank to confirm the L/C).

Part II Sample Letters

Sample 1 Requesting Payment by D/A

Dear Sirs,

Thank you for your letter of May 8 concerning your new product, Smart Choice. We take great interest in your product and wish to discuss further about it.

It is noted that you require letter of credit for the payment. However, we would like to propose payment by D/A for our first order, as this is a new product and we are not able to make purchase on our own account. You can rest assured that we will place substantial orders once the demand for this product has been ascertained.

We believe our proposal is a reasonable way to test the market and hope you will be willing to cooperate with us.

Yours faithfully,

Notes
1. take great interest in 兴趣很浓厚
   We take great interest in your products and wish to have quotations for the items specified below.
   我们对贵公司产品感兴趣，并希望得到下列产品的报价。
2. on one's own account 自费地，自担风险地
   We shall insure the contracted goods on our own account.
   我们将为合同货物投保，费用由我方自理。
3. ascertain v. 确定，查明
   The debt auction is critical to ascertain market demand for Portuguese bonds.
   债券拍卖对稳定葡萄牙债券的市场需求至关重要。

Sample 2 Proposing to Pay by 30 Days L/C

Dear Sirs,

We have pleasure in placing with you an order for 1,000 M/T of Mild Steel Bars at your price of US $ 400 per M/T CIF HK for shipment during November.

For this particular order we would like to pay by 30 days L/C. Involving about US $ 400,000, this order is comparatively a big one. As we have only moderate means at hand, the tie-up of funds for as long as three to four months indeed presents a problem to us.

We very much appreciate the support you have extended us in the past. If you can accommodate us this time, please send us your contract, upon receipt of which we will establish the relevant L/C immediately.

Yours faithfully,

Notes
1. 30 days L/C 见票后30天议付的信用证
2. moderate adj. 适度的，不大的，中等的

    moderate means 财力有限
  3. extend *v.* =offer, grant, accord 给予，施与

Sample 3 Reply

Dear Sirs,

Thank you for your order of Mild Steel Bars as per your letter of August 8.

Your proposal of paying by L/C at 30 days has been carefully studied by us. Usually, time credit is not acceptable to us. However, in view of our long pleasant relations, we agree with you this time. But let us make it clear that this accommodation is only for this transaction, which will, in no case, set a precedent.

Attached hereto is our Sales Confirmation No. SC223 covering the above order. Please follow the usual procedure.

Yours faithfully,

Notes
  1. accommodation *n.* 照顾；通融
    This accommodation is only for this transaction, which will, in no case, set a precedent. 这次通融仅限于此笔交易，下不为例。
  2. time credit = time L/C 远期信用证

Sample 4 Modifying Terms of Payment

Dear Sirs,

We have studied the specifications and pricelist of your new colour TV sets and now wish to place the enclosed order with you. As we are in urgent need of several of the items, we should be obliged if you could make up and ship the order as soon as you possibly can.

In the past we have dealt with you on sight credit basis. Now, we would like to propose a different way of payment, i.e. when the goods purchased by us are ready for shipment and the freight space booked, you cable us and we will remit you the full amount by T/T. The reasons are that we can thus more confidently assure our buyers of the time of delivery and save a lot of expenses on opening the letter of credit. As we feel this would not make much difference to you but would facilitate our sales, we hope you will grant our request.

We look forward to your confirmation of our order and your affirmative reply to our new arrangements of payment.

Yours faithfully,

Notes
1. to make up sth. 拼凑成，配齐
2. remit v. 汇寄，汇款
   remittance n. 汇款；汇付

Sample 5　Asking for Easier Payment Terms

Dear Sirs,

Our past purchase of bicycles from you has been paid as a rule by confirmed, irrevocable letter of credit.

On this basis, it has indeed cost us a great deal. From the moment we open credit till the time our buyers pay us, the tie-up of our funds lasts about four months. Under the present circumstances, this question is particularly taxing owing to the tight money condition and unprecedented high bank interest.

If you would kindly make easier payment terms, we are sure that such an accommodation would be conducive to encouraging business. We propose either "Cash against Documents on arrival of goods" or "Drawing on us at three months' sight."

Your kindness in giving priority to the consideration of the above request and giving us an early favourable reply will be highly appreciated.

Yours faithfully,

Notes
1. unprecedented high bank interest 前所未有的银行高利息
2. cash against document on arrival of goods 货到后凭单付款
3. draw on us at three months' sight 开出见票三个月付款的汇票向我们收款

Sample 6　Reply

Dear Sirs,

　　We note from your letter of August 2 that you wish to ask for an extension of our terms.

　　Actually, there is nothing unusual in our original arrangement. Counting from the time you open credit till the time shipment reaches your port, the interval, which is quite normal, is only about three months. Besides, your L/C is opened when the goods are ready for shipment. In this case, we are sorry that we cannot meet your wishes.

As we must adhere to our customary practice, we sincerely hope that you will not think us unaccommodating.

As soon as a fresh supply of bicycles comes in, we will contact you.

Yours faithfully,

Notes
1. unaccommodating *adj.* 不肯通融的，不肯照顾的
2. a fresh supply 新货源

Part III Reading Materials

What Is an Exchange Rate?
An exchange rate is the rate at which one currency can be exchanged for another. In other words, it is the value of another country's currency compared to that of your own. If you are traveling to another country, you need to "buy" the local currency. Just like the price of any asset, the exchange rate is the price at which you can buy that currency. If you are traveling to Egypt, for example, and the exchange rate for U.S. dollars is 1:5.5 Egyptian pounds, this means that for every U.S. dollar, you can buy five and a half Egyptian pounds. Theoretically, identical assets should sell at the same price in different countries, because the exchange rate must maintain the inherent value of one currency against the other.

Fixed Exchange Rates①
There are two ways the price of a currency can be determined against another. A fixed, or pegged, rate is a rate the government (central bank) sets and maintains as the official exchange rate. A set price will be determined against a major world currency (usually the U.S. dollar, but also other major currencies such as the euro, the yen or a basket of currencies). In order to maintain the local exchange rate, the central bank buys and sells its own currency on the foreign exchange market in return for the currency to which it is pegged.

If, for example, it is determined that the value of a single unit of local currency is equal to US$3, the central bank will have to ensure that it can supply the market with those dollars. In order to maintain the rate, the central bank must keep a high level of foreign reserves. This is a reserved amount of foreign currency held by the central bank that it can use to release (or absorb) extra funds into (or out of) the market. This ensures an appropriate money supply, appropriate fluctuations in the market (inflation/deflation④) and ultimately, the exchange rate. The central bank can also adjust the official exchange rate when necessary.

Floating Exchange Rates[2]

Unlike the fixed rate, a floating exchange rate is determined by the private market through supply and demand. A floating rate is often termed "self-correcting," as any differences in supply and demand will automatically be corrected in the market. Look at this simplified model: if demand for a currency is low, its value will decrease, thus making imported goods more expensive and stimulating demand for local goods and services. This in turn will generate more jobs, causing an auto-correction in the market. A floating exchange rate is constantly changing.

In reality, no currency is wholly fixed or floating. In a fixed regime, market pressures can also influence changes in the exchange rate. Sometimes, when a local currency reflects its true value against its pegged currency, a "black market" (which is more reflective of actual supply and demand) may develop. A central bank will often then be forced to revalue or devalue[5] the official rate so that the rate is in line with the unofficial one, thereby halting the activity of the black market.

In a floating regime, the central bank may also intervene when it is necessary to ensure stability and to avoid inflation. However, it is less often that the central bank of a floating regime will interfere.

The World Once Pegged[3]

Between 1870 and 1914, there was a global fixed exchange rate. Currencies were linked to gold, meaning that the value of a local currency was fixed at a set exchange rate to gold ounces. This was known as the gold standard. This allowed for unrestricted capital mobility as well as global stability in currencies and trade. However, with the start of World War I, the gold standard was abandoned.

At the end of World War II, the conference at Bretton Woods, an effort to generate global economic stability and increase global trade, established the basic rules and regulations governing international exchange. As such, an international monetary system, embodied in the International Monetary Fund (IMF)[6], was established to promote foreign trade and to maintain the monetary stability of countries and therefore, that of the global economy.

It was agreed that currencies would once again be fixed, or pegged, but this time to the U.S. dollar, which in turn was pegged to gold at US$35 per ounce. What this meant was that the value of a currency was directly linked with the value of the U.S. dollar. So, if you needed to buy Japanese yen, the value of the yen would be expressed in U.S. dollars, whose value in turn was determined in the value of gold. If a country needed to readjust the value of its currency, it could approach the IMF to adjust the pegged value of its currency. The peg was maintained until 1971, when the U.S. dollar could no longer hold the value of the pegged rate of US$35 per ounce of gold.

From then on, major governments adopted a floating system, and all attempts to move back to a global peg were eventually abandoned in 1985. Since then, no major economies have gone back to a peg, and the use of gold as a peg has been completely abandoned.

Why Peg?

The reasons to peg a currency are linked to stability. Especially in today's developing nations, a country may decide to peg its currency to create a stable atmosphere for foreign investment. With a peg, the investor will always know what his or her investment's value is, and, therefore, will not have to worry about daily fluctuations⑦. A pegged currency can also help to lower inflation rates and generate demand, which results from greater confidence in the stability of the currency.

Fixed regimes, however, can often lead to severe financial crises, since a peg is difficult to maintain in the long run. This was seen in the Mexican (1995), Asian (1997) and Russian (1997) financial crises: an attempt to maintain a high value of the local currency to the peg resulted in the currencies eventually becoming overvalued. This meant that the governments could no longer meet the demands to convert the local currency into the foreign currency at the pegged rate. With speculation and panic, investors scrambled to get their money out and convert it into foreign currency before the local currency was devalued against the peg; foreign reserve supplies⑧ eventually became depleted. In Mexico's case, the government was forced to devalue the peso by 30%. In Thailand, the government eventually had to allow the currency to float, and by the end of 1997, the Thai baht had lost 50% of its value as the market's demand and supply readjusted the value of the local currency.

Countries with pegs are often associated with having unsophisticated capital markets and weak regulating institutions. The peg is there to help create stability in such an environment. It takes a stronger system as well as a mature market to maintain a float. When a country is forced to devalue its currency, it is also required to proceed with some form of economic reform, like implementing greater transparency, in an effort to strengthen its financial institutions.

Some governments may choose to have a "floating" or "crawling" peg, whereby the government reassesses the value of the peg periodically and then changes the peg rate accordingly. Usually, this causes devaluation, but it is controlled to avoid market panic. This method is often used in the transition from a peg to a floating regime, and it allows the government to "save face" by not being forced to devalue in an uncontrollable crisis.

The Bottom Line

Although the peg has worked in creating global trade and monetary stability, it was used only at a time when all the major economies were a part of it. While a floating regime is not without its flaws, it has proven to be a more efficient means of determining the long-term value of a currency and creating equilibrium in the international market.

Notes
① fixed exchange rate 固定汇率
② floating exchange rate 浮动汇率
③ peg v. 固定(价格、数量等)
④ inflation n. 通货膨胀
   deflation n. 通货紧缩
⑤ devalue v. = devaluate 使(货币)贬值

devaluation *n.* 货币贬值
⑥ the International Monetary Fund /IMF 国际货币基金组织
⑦ fluctuation *n.* 波动；fluctuation of exchange rate 汇率波动
⑧ foreign reserve supply 外汇储备供应

 Questions

1. What are the two ways of determining the price of one currency against another? What are the merits of both ways?
2. When and how was the international exchange rate pegged?
3. Why did countries attempt to get their currencies pegged?

> 汇率与一国的经济紧密相关，影响到该国进出口业务、进口商品的物价及资本的流动。一国货币汇率的稳定与否，集中反映了该国的经济实力及其在国际竞争中的地位。人民币币值的稳定，将有效地保障中国改革开放的顺利进行和经济持续发展，维护良好的国际形象。

Exercises

I. Fill in the blanks with the best choice:

1. As usual, we are _____ on you at 30 days in favour of HSBC Bank for the value of the consignments and trust you will accept our draft upon _____.
   a. collecting, documentation b. drawing, presentation
   c. remitting, presentation   d. paying, documentation
2. If the amount _____ that figure, an L/C is required.
   a. involves   b. covers
   c. exceeds   d. prevails
3. In view of the amount of this transaction being very small, we are prepared to accept payment by _____ for the value of the goods shipped.
   a. D/P at sight   b. L/C at sight
   c. B/L   d. S/C
4. As this is a very big order, we must adhere to our customary practice and require payment by _____.
   a. T/T   b. D/A
   c. L/C at sight   d. D/P at 30 days
5. We very much regret that we are unable to accept any fresh orders at present owing to heavy _____.
   a. commitments   b. consignments
   c. accommodations d. premium
6. We propose to turn the whole lot over to you, once for all, with a 20% discount _____ their list price.
   a. in   b. off   c. at   d. from

7. If the amount involved in a transaction is relatively big, the often suggested payment method is _____.
   a. L/C at sight   b. Bill of Exchange
   c. collection   d. cash

8. We have drawn on you for this amount at 60 days sight, _____ the shipping documents.
   a. enclosing   b. including
   c. attaching   d. covering

9. We fax you this morning, _____ you an order _____ 2000 colour TV sets.
   a. putting; for   b. sending; of
   c. taking; of   d. placing; for

10. We very much appreciate it if you can _____ us this time.
    a. consider   b. extend
    c. accommodate   d. facilitate

II. Translate the following sentences into English:

1. 请注意，付款是以保兑的、不可撤销的、允许分装和转船、见票即付的信用证支付。
2. 你方的付款交单要求，我方已予考虑，鉴于这笔交易金额甚微，我们准备以此方式办理装运。
3. 按照你方要求，我们破例接受以30天迟期信用证办理交货，但下不为例。
4. 如果你方能惠予较宽松的条件，我们将非常感激。
5. 我们非常高兴地通知你方，上述合同项下货物已备妥待运。请电汇全部货款。
6. 对这笔交易，我方已开即期汇票向你方收款。
7. 我方已向你方解释清楚，信用证必须在本月底前开到，以便赶装下月15日开往你港的"东风"轮。
8. 鉴于我们多年的良好业务关系，我们同意做出让步，相信这将满足你方的要求。
9. 我们相信这一通融将使你方为我们获得更多的订单。
10. 抱歉我方不能接受货到目的港后凭单付款的支付方式。

III. Translate the following sentences into Chinese:

1. We have drawn on you for this amount at sight through the HSBC Bank, who has been instructed to hand over documents against payment of the draft.
2. It will interest you to know that as a special sign of encouragement, we shall consider accepting payment by D/P during this sales-pushing stage.
3. We would suggest that for this particular order you let us have a D/D, on receipt of which we shall ship the goods on the first available steamer.
4. We hope you will accommodate us in this respect and look forward to your favourable reply.
5. As agreed, the terms of payment for the above orders are letters of credit at 60 days' sight or D/P sight draft.
6. In view of our friendly cooperation, we are prepared to accept payment by D/P at 60 days' sight.
7. We regret to inform you that it is our usual practice not to accept payment by D/A.

8. Please see to it that you will establish the covering L/C as soon as possible so as to enable us to effect shipment within the stipulated time limit.
9. Yesterday I did remit you US $3,000 and will remit you US $5,000 shortly. The balance I would try to remit you on time.
10. The documentary credit is available against presentation of the following documents.

IV. Letter writing:

Write a letter to ask the seller for an accommodation to the usual payment terms of sight L/C. You may refer to some of the following details:
1. The transaction is big, involving US $ 500,000;
2. The cost of sight L/C is high;
3. Moderate means at hand;
4. Tie-up of funds for three or four months;
5. Long and friendly cooperation in the past;
6. D/P is preferred.

chapter Seven

Establishment of and Amendment to L/C

Part I Introduction

Payment either by remittance or by collection depends on the commercial credit of the exporter and the importer. While, under L/C, it is the bank credit that both parties count on. This solves the possible problems arising from the distrust between the exporter and the importer, as an L/C enables the exporter to draw on a named bank when he presents the required documents. Thus, under L/C, the exporter can feel assured that so long as he has made the delivery of the goods and got the required documents, he can get the payment of the goods in due course and the importer can also feel at ease that he can get the shipping documents when he effects the payment of the goods.

The chief contents of the L/C can be seen as a combination of the chief contents of the sales contract, the required documents and the bank assurance. The L/C must state the maximum amount and the duration of the credit, the usance (the term) of the draft and the shipping documents that are to be sent with the draft.

In receipt of the L/C, the exporter must make sure that all the terms and conditions in the credit can be complied with and if not, amendments should be made well in advance of shipment of the goods. Otherwise, the exporter may run the risk of his draft being dishonoured by the bank.

Procedures of L/C Payment

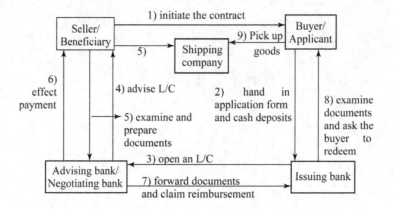

- After a sales contract is initiated, the importer and the exporter agree to have payment settled by means of L/C.
- The applicant (importer) will first request the issuing bank to issue an L/C, usually an irrevocable documentary L/C, in favor of the beneficiary (exporter).
- The issuing bank will examine the credit-worthiness of the importer before it considers issuing the L/C.
- The L/C issued by the bank is then passed to the advising bank (the exporter's bank) that represents the beneficiary in his country.
- On receiving the L/C, the exporter will check the terms and conditions against the sales contract to ensure that everything agrees with the credit requirement.
- Then the exporter will forward all the documents required by credit to the advising bank or negotiating bank to get payment.
- The issuing bank will check the documents against the terms and conditions of the L/C.
- The exporter, after receiving the L/C from the importer, should first of all go through all the clauses set forth in the L/C to make sure they are in full conformity with the terms stipulated in the sales contract.
- When some discrepancies or some soft clauses which the beneficiary does not agree to accept are included in the L/C, the exporter shall notify the importer to amend the L/C.
- Then the importer will ask the issuing bank to send notification of amendment to the beneficiary.
- Besides the buyer, the exporter can also request to amend the L/C. After obtaining the consent from the seller, he can instruct the issuing bank to make amendment.

Part II Sample Letters

Sample 1 A Specimen of an L/C

THE BANK OF TOKYO, LTD. New York Agency 100 Broadway New York, N. Y. 10005		
DOCUMENTARY CREDITS DEPARTMENT		Date: 20th July, 2011
IRREVOCABLE DOCUMENTARY CREDIT	Credit number of issuing bank 110 LCI 985467	Of advising bank
Advising bank Pre-advised by: Telex Through Bank of China, Qingdao, China	**Applicant** Kanematsu-Gosho (Canada) Inc. 400 de Maisonneuve Blvd. W. Montreal, Quebec	

Beneficiary	Amount
China National Textiles Imp. & Exp. Corp. 78 Jiangxi Road, Qingdao, China	Abt. CAD 174,000 (ABOUT CANADIAN DOLLARS ONE HUNDRED SEVENTY FOUR THOUSAND ONLY)
	Expiry For negotiation on August 16, 2011

Dear Sirs,

We hereby issue the Irrevocable Documentary Letter of Credit which is available by beneficiary's drafts on us for full invoice value at sight bearing the credit number and date of issue, and accompanied by the following documents:

1. Signed Commercial Invoice in triplicate;
2. Full set of Clean on Board Bills of Lading issued to order of shipper marked "Freight Prepaid" and notify accountee;
3. Insurance Policy or Certificate in duplicate, covering Marine and War Risks up to buyer's warehouse, for the invoice value of the goods plus10%;
4. Packing List in triplicate;
5. Weight and Measurement Certificate in triplicate.

Evidencing shipment of:
About 300,000 yards of 65% Polyester, 35% Cotton Grey Lawn as per buyer's order,
No. S- 0534,
CFR Montreal.

We are informed insurance is to be covered by buyer.

Shipment from China to Montreal latest July 31, 2011.	Partial shipment permitted
	Transshipment permitted

All other bank charges are for the account of beneficiary.
Documents must be presented to negotiating bank or paying bank within 15 days after the on board date of Bills of Lading, but within validity of letter of credit.
Special Conditions:
Two sets of non-negotiable shipping documents must be airmailed to Kanematsu-Gosho (Canada) Inc., Montreal and beneficiary's certificate to this effect is required.
Special Instructions for Reimbursement:
We will pay the negotiating bank as per their instructions upon receipt of documents.
The amount of any draft drawn under this credit must, concurrently with negotiation, be endorsed on the reverse hereof, and the presentment of any such draft shall be a warranty by the negotiating bank that such endorsement has been made and that documents have been forwarded as herein required.
We hereby engage with the drawers, endorsers and bona fide holders of drafts drawn and negotiated under and in compliance with the terms of this credit that the same shall be duly honoured on due presentation to the drawee.
The advising bank is requested to notify the beneficiary without adding their confirmation.

Yours faithfully,
Co-signed (signature No.9247)   Signed (signature No/02467)
RF202 replacing RE.83.606 series

PLEASE SEE REVERSE

Sample 2 Urging Establishment of L/C

Dear Sirs,

With reference to 35,000 yards of Cotton Piece Goods under the Sales Contract No. SC520 signed at the Autumn Fair, we would like to draw your attention to the fact that the date of delivery is approaching, but up to now we have not received your relative letter of credit. Would you kindly open an L/C before 30th of this month, so that we can execute the order within the period of shipment. Otherwise, the time of shipment will be postponed.

In order to avoid subsequent amendments, please see to it that the stipulations of the L/C are in strict accordance with the terms of the Sales Contract.

Looking forward to your early reply.

Yours faithfully,

Notes
1. Cotton Piece Goods 棉制品
2. the Autumn Fair 秋季交易会
3. execute v. 执行，实施
   execute order 执行订单
4. in accordance with =in agreement or conformity with 依照，根据，与……一致

Sample 3 Urging Establishment of L/C

Dear Sirs,

As regards our Sales Confirmation No. 965 dated June 7, we regret to say that your letter of credit has not yet reached us. This has caused us much inconvenience as we have already made preparations for shipment according to the terms of the Sales Confirmation.

Actually, the goods you ordered have been ready for quite some time and the demand lately has been so great that we find it difficult to keep them for you any longer. However, in consideration of our friendly business relations, we are prepared to await your L/C, which must reach us not later than October 15. If we again fail to receive your L/C in time, we shall cancel our Sales Confirmation and you will be asked to refund to us the storage charges we have paid on your behalf.

Looking forward to your early reply. Your cooperation in this matter will be appreciated.

Yours sincerely,

Notes

1. cause much inconvenience 带来诸多不便
2. refund to us the storage charges 退还我方仓储费用

Sample 4   Advising the Establishment of L/C

Dear Sirs,

We wish to invite your attention to our Order No. 6231 covering 500 pieces of Pongee Silk, for which we sent to you about 30 days ago a confirmed, irrevocable L/C in your favour, expiring on May 15.

As the season is drawing near, our buyers are in urgent need of the goods. It will be greatly appreciated if you effect shipment as soon as possible, thus enabling them to catch the brisk demand at the start of the season.

We would like to stress that any delay in shipping our order will undoubtedly involve us in no small difficulty.

Thank you in advance for your cooperation.

Yours faithfully,

Notes

1. expire *v.* 期满，到期，终止
   The import license expires on September 11.
   进口许可证9月11日到期。
   His term of office as President expires next year.
   他的总统任期明年截止。
   expiry *n.* 期满
2. brisk *adj.* 活跃的，兴旺的
   catch the brisk demand 赶上旺盛的需求
   The market is brisk.
   市场兴旺。
   There is a brisk demand for cell phones.
   对手机的需求旺盛。

Sample 5   Amending L/C to Allow Partial Shipment and Transshipment

Dear Sirs,

Letter of Credit No. 5687 issued by the HSBC Bank has duly arrived. On perusal, we find that transshipment and partial shipment are not allowed.

As direct steamers to your port are few and far between, we have to ship via Hong Kong more often than not. As to partial shipment, it would be to our mutual benefit if we could ship immediately whatever is ready instead of waiting for the whole shipment to be completed. Therefore, we have emailed you this afternoon, asking you to amend your L/C to read "Part shipments and transshipment allowed."

We hope you will see to it that the amendment is effected without delay.

Yours faithfully,

Notes
1. amend *v.* 修正，改正
   amend L/C 修改信用证
   amend the term of packing 修改包装条款
   amend the amount of L/C 修改信用证金额
   amend the negotiation date of the L/C 修改信用证议付期
2. perusal *n.* 细读
   on perusal 经仔细阅读，经详阅
3. via *prep.* 经由
4. more often than not 经常，多半
5. The amendment is effected without delay.
   速改信用证/立即修改信用证。

Sample 6 Amending the Amount and Packing Terms

Dear Sirs,

<u>Re: L/C No.85 Issued by First National City Bank</u>

We have received the above L/C established by you in payment for your Order No. B201 covering 300 cases of iron nail.

When we checked the L/C with the relevant contract, we found that the amount in your L/C is insufficient. The correct total CIF New York value of your order comes to US $ 2,800 instead of US $ 2,600, the difference being US $ 200.

Your L/C allows us only half a month to effect delivery. But when we signed the contract we have agreed that the delivery should be made within one month upon receipt of the Letter of Credit.

As to packing, the contract stipulates that the goods should be packed in cartons and reinforced with nylon straps outside, but your L/C required metal straps instead. We think we should arrange the packing according to the contract.

In view of the above, you are kindly requested to increase the amount of your L/C by US $200, extend the shipment and validity to September 15 and 30 respectively, and amend the term of packing as well. Meanwhile, please advise us by fax.

Your early amendment will be appreciated.

Yours faithfully,

Notes
1. The amount in your L/C is insufficient.
   信用证所开金额不足。
2. to effect delivery 发货
3. stipulate *v.* 规定，保证
4. reinforce *v.* 加强，加固
5. nylon strap 尼龙带（绳）
6. respectively *adv.* 分别地，各个地

Sample 7 Asking for Extension of L/C

Dear Sirs,

L/C No. UK2563

As stipulated in S/C 90TX-256, shipment could be made in July provided your L/C reached us not later than 15th of June. However, we received your L/C only yesterday and it is absolutely impossible for us to ship the goods in July.

Under such a circumstances, we regret to have to ask you to extend the above L/C to August 31 and September 15 for shipment and negotiation respectively, with the amendment reaching us by July 15; otherwise, shipment will be further postponed.

We look forward to receiving the relevant amendment at an early date and thank you in advance.

Yours faithfully,

Notes
1. shipment and negotiation 装运期及信用证议付期
2. Shipment will be further postponed. 装运期将进一步延误（推迟）。

Sample 8 Reply

Dear Sirs,

<u>L/C No. UK2563</u>

We have received your letter of June 30 requesting us to extend the above L/C to the August 31st and September 15th for shipment and negotiation respectively.

We are quite aware of the conditions set forth in S/C 90TX-256 that the goods ordered could be shipped in July only if the covering L/C reached you on June 15 at the latest. However, as we had to go through the necessary formalities of applying for the relevant import license, we could not open the L/C earlier. The import license was granted on June 17 and is valid only up to July 31.

We are willing to do whatever we can to cooperate with you, but as the present import regulations do not allow any extension of license, we regret to have to say that it is beyond our ability to meet your request to extend the above L/C.

Please do your best to ship the goods in time and we thank you for your cooperation.

Yours faithfully,

Notes
1. set forth 宣布，陈述，阐明
2. go through 办理
3. formality n. 手续
4. import license 进口许可证
5. extension of import license 进口许可证展期

Part III Reading Materials

What is commercial credit?

Sometimes referred to as business credit or commercial lending①, commercial credit has to do with the ability of a business to obtain goods and services from a supplier. Business credit is extended with the understanding that the business promises to pay the supplier according to the terms and conditions that the buyer agreed to at the time of acquisition.

The range of goods and services that are covered under the concept of business credit extend beyond supplies and similar types of purchases. Commercial credit also has to do with the securing of bank loans. When seeking a bank loan from a qualified lender, there are a number of different factors that go into determining the level of commercial credit that will be extended. Among those factors are the current worth of the holdings② in the possession of the applicant, the current ratio of cash assets③ to outstanding indebtedness④, and the worth of assets that could be converted into cash easily or used as collateral⑤ for the loan. The credit history of the corporation will also be taken into account. Once the financial profile⑥ is complete, the lender will determine the amount of commercial credit that can be extended to the corporation.

Protecting the commercial credit is one of the most important tasks that face modern companies. The ability to obtain financial assistance, or to secure goods and services that will enhance the operation of the company, forms the basis for continued growth in many industries today. Failure to maintain a good financial rating will result in the decrease of the extension of commercial credit, and in some cases can cause a lender to revoke the privilege altogether.

The judicious use of commercial credit ensures that a corporation has resources to call upon when a temporary downturn in sales takes place, or when an opportunity to expand operations in order to take advantage of market changes takes place. Under the right conditions, companies can prosper, increasing their commercial credit rating⑦ in the process.

What is a credit circle?

Large industries, particularly those involved in distribution of goods, regularly extend credit agreements to their customers. These agreements are often among the distributor and other businesses and can involve very large sums of money. As several competing businesses within an industry may have dealings with the same client, it is beneficial for all those companies to know the payment practices of that client. Often, these companies will create a credit circle as a means of sharing that information.

A credit circle offers additional advantages to a traditional credit check. Most importantly, the circle can have access to information about a customer's missed payments without the 30-to 90-day lag that is common in credit-reporting agencies⑧. In addition, credit managers often notice subtleties that would not be reported to credit agencies. For example, if a company historically paid its debts in full each month but has begun only paying a percentage, it would be an indicator of financial stress that could be otherwise overlooked.

It is common for a credit circle to meet frequently, sometimes as many as 6 to 12 times a year. In addition, members of the group have a responsibility to alert others if the typical payment pattern of a common customer suddenly changes. The other members of the circle are then in the position to assess and limit their own risk.

As a credit circle is composed of several competing business, great care should be taken by the group to avoid unethical or even illegal behaviors. Several statutes, including The United Kingdom's 1998 Competition Act, have been enacted to prevent economically harmful and unfair business practices. These laws have established what can and cannot be discussed or agreed upon by the members of credit circles.

Members of credit circles may offer information regarding the specifics of a debtor's payments; they cannot, however, offer opinions on whether or not that debtor should be given credit by other companies. Likewise, customer credit limits and the terms of credit arrangements may not be discussed. In essence, credit circles cannot establish a distributor-wide total credit line for a particular customer.

Additionally, members of a credit circle are prohibited from forming any agreement among members that would provide an unfair business advantage or discourage competition. Agreements to standardize industry prices or employee wages are expressly forbidden. Furthermore, the credit circle as a whole cannot make a joint decision to deny business to any group or individual.

What are the benefits of letters of credit?

A letter of credit allows a company to substitute a bank's credit for its own in a business transaction. The benefits of letters of credit include helping a company complete a business transaction without the use of cash or another form of payment. Another benefit is the completion of international business transactions that might be quite complex. The secondary benefits of letters of credit include flexibility, because there are two main types of letters: commercial and standby. A company can secure either type, depending on its need.

Commercial letters of credit[①] are mostly a method to facilitate payments in an international business transaction. The letter acts as a contract between the bank writing the letter and another bank. The benefits of letters of credit for this purpose include allowing the second bank to make payments to a beneficiary. The beneficiary typically is the business providing the goods or services. For international transactions, the second bank might be in another country, allowing the transaction to go smoothly.

A standby letter of credit[②] is slightly different. This letter of credit acts as a secondary payment system, outside of the primary payment system of cash or credit. Letters of credit written in the standby format are not actually going to be forms of payment. The letter simply states that the company has the ability to pay through a bank if the business cannot pay through a primary method. Essentially, the standby letter of credit shows a company's creditworthiness in the business market.

Outside of these specific benefits to each letter of credit, other benefits of letters of credit exist. In most cases, the letters are negotiable. The bank issuing the letter might not actually pay but might allow its customer to transfer the note to another party. Revocable letters of credit can have changes or adjustments made to the language in the letter. Letters might also be a sight or time draft; sight drafts are payable upon presenting the letter to the bank, and a time draft pays only after a specific time period.

Though letters of credit are quite common, all businesses are not always able to secure them. The benefits of letters of credit come only to businesses that can be good customers for issuing banks. These companies are often large and have multiple payment methods. The letter of credit simply allows them to avoid initial cash payments for transactions. A letter of credit might last for a certain time period, so the business could use it repeatedly.

Notes

① commercial lending 商业贷款

② holdings *n.* 所持股份
③ cash assets 现金资产
④ indebtedness *n.* 债务
⑤ collateral *n.* 抵押品
⑥ the financial profile 财务状况
⑦ credit rating 信用评级
⑧ credit-reporting agencies 信贷报告机构
⑨ a commercial letter of credit 商业信用证
⑩ a standby letter of credit 备用信用证

Questions

1. What is a commercial credit? How is it related to companies?
2. What parties does a credit circle comprise? What are they prohibited from doing?
3. What are the benefits of letters of credit?

Exercises

I. Fill in the blanks with the best choice:

1. We would like to stress that the L/C stipulations must be _____ with the terms of the S/C.
   a. in exact accordance with   b. in full reference to
   c. in exact view of   d. in full light of

2. Please note that the goods _____ our S/C No. 563 are now ready for shipment.
   a. about   b. under
   c. in   d. of

3. We have opened an irrevocable and confirmed L/C _____ Bank of China.
   a. in   b. by
   c. with   d. for

4. Your L/C No. 253 is to be established _____ the amount of HK$50,000.
   a. for   b. with
   c. at   d. on

5. We hereby undertake to _____ all drafts drawn in accordance with the terms of the above credit.
   a. hounour   b. pay
   c. refund   d. credit

6. The payment method for this particular transaction is confirmed, irrevocable L/C by seller's documentary draft at sight _____ for negotiation in China until 15 days after date of shipment.
   a. used   b. presented
   c. valid   d. collected

7. The L/C must reach the sellers 30 days before the contracted date of _____.
   a. payment   b. shipment
   c. arrival   d. transportation
8. The beneficiary's draft shall be drawn against the L/C _____ by the following documents.
   a. accompanied   b. companied
   c. companying   d. accompanying
9. You must be responsible for all the losses _____ from your delay in opening the covering L/C.
   a. arousing   b. rising
   c. arising   d. have arisen
10. The chief contents of the L/C is a combination of the chief contents of the sales contract, the _____ and the bank assurance.
    a. bill of lading   b. bill of exchange
    c. commercial invoice   d. required documents

II. Translate the following sentences into English:
1. 请注意第535号合同下10,000台缝纫机备妥待运已久，但我们至今尚未收到你方有关信用证。请速开证，以便装运。
2. 兹通知你方，以你方为受益人、不可撤销的、保兑的信用证已由中国银行开出。
3. 如你方能立即办理改证并通知我方，将不胜感激。
4. 请注意（做到）信用证条款必须与合同条款完全一致。
5. 由于你方信用证装运期与有效期相同，我们在装运后没有足够的时间办理单据结汇，故请按惯例将该信用证有效期延展15天。
6. 你方第568号信用证已收到，但经详阅后发现不准转船和分批装运，请立即修改你们的信用证。
7. 我方将由香港汇丰银行开出即期汇票向你方收取该笔款项。
8. 只要你方提出，我们愿给你方60天的展期，并真诚地希望此举能有助于你们摆脱当前困境。
9. 非常遗憾，尽管我们提出了请求，但信用证仍未作必要修改。
10. 我们今天给你方发去传真，要求你们将信用证256号作如下修改："由上海港装运"改为"由青岛港装运"；"长吨"改为"吨"。

III. Translate the following sentences into Chinese:
1. We have received your L/C No. 562, but we find it contains the following discrepancies: ... We would, therefore, request you to instruct your bankers to make the necessary amendment.
2. As there is no direct liner from Qingdao to your port during June/July, it is imperative for you to delete the clause "By direct steamer" and insert "Partial shipments and transshipment are allowed."
3. The buyers insist that an irrevocable L/C be opened within ten days after the receipt of the sellers' advice that the goods are ready for shipment.
4. We hereby undertake to honour all drafts drawn in accordance with the terms of the above credit.

5. Please amend your L/C No. 256 to include the wording: "5% more or less" under the items of quantity and amount.
6. In order to pave the way for your pushing the sale of our products in your market, we will accept payment by D/P at sight as a special accommodation.
7. As you have failed to establish in time the L/C covering our sales confirmation No. 1033, we have to rescind the sales confirmation and hold you responsible for all the losses arising therefrom.
8. The commission allowed for this transaction is 3% as clearly stipulated in our Contract No. 146, but we find that your L/C No. 557 demands a commission of 5%. This is obviously not in line with the contract stipulations. We shall, therefore, be grateful if you will instruct your bankers to amend the L/C to read "commission 3%."
9. It has been our usual practice to do business with payment by D/A at sight instead of by L/C. We should, therefore, like you to accept D/A terms for this transaction and future ones.
10. Much to our regret, we are unable to comply with your request for an extension to our L/C No.225, the reason being that the present import regulations do not permit any extension of import licenses.

IV. Letter writing:

Write a letter to ask the buyer to extend the L/C. You may refer to some of the following details:

1. The L/C arrived two weeks late on the 13th of August;
2. Only one vessel sailing for the destination port every month and the sailing date usually in the early half of a month;
3. The only vessel sailing for the destination port this month is to depart in two days' time, and the shipping space has been fully booked;
4. Shipment and negotiation dates to be extended to 14th and 30th of September respectively.

Chapter Eight

Shipment

Part I Introduction

1. Overview

Shipment is one of the indispensable terms of a sales contract. Upon the conclusion of a contract, the party responsible for the arrangement of shipment as provided under the contract will have to perform his obligation of making shipping arrangements. In practice, shipment involves such procedures as clearing the goods through the customs, booking shipping space or chartering a ship, completing shipping documentation, dispatching shipping advices, etc.

Before shipment, the buyers generally send their shipping requirements to the sellers, informing them in writing of the packing and marks, mode of transportation, etc., known as the Shipping Instructions. On the other hand, the sellers (or the exporter) usually send a notice to the buyers immediately after the goods are loaded on board the ship, advising them of the shipment, especially under FOB or CFR terms. Such a notice, known as the Shipping Advice, may include the following: Contract and/ or L/C No., name of the commodity, number of packages, total quantity shipped, name of vessel and its sailing date and sometimes even the total value of the goods.

Export transportation involves a lot of complicated procedures. Before the goods are to be dispatched, the following must be duly seen to:
- send the Shipping instructions by the buyer;
- select a shipping line and a particular vessel;
- book shipping space or chartering and sign the contract of carriage;
- register the cargo on shipping note and send the shipping note to a shipping company;
- register details on customs, entry forms and send them to Customs;
- arrange adequate packing, including shipping marks;
- receive the bill of lading from the shipping company;
- pay the freight bill;
- arrange the shipment;
- send the shipping documents and Shipping Advice.

Terms of shipment generally contain time of shipment, ports of shipment and destination, transshipment and partial shipment, shipping documents and so on.

2. Time of Shipment

To stipulate the time of delivery when the parties are concluding a contract, both parties have to think of many links and elements for the implementation of the sales contract such as the time needed for the seller to get the contracted goods ready or for the buyer to get import license, etc. In the contract, several ways are used to state the time of delivery:

- A definite time is given for shipment. For example: Shipment during January; Shipment on or before July 15.
- When the payment is made by L/C, the time of shipment is usually made in connection with the time of receipt of L/C. For instance The L/C must reach the seller not later than July 15th, and shipment must be made within 30 days after receipt of L/C.
- Recent shipment. When the shipment can be made soon after the conclusion of the contract, the parties can adopt such terms: immediate shipment, prompt shipment, shipment as soon as possible, etc.

3. Partial Shipment and Transshipment

In case of an export covering a large quantity of goods, it is necessary to make shipment in several lots by several carriers sailing on different dates. This is done owing to limitation of shipping space available, port unloading facilities at the port of destination, dull market season, or possible delay in the process of manufacturing the goods, etc. Partial shipment is allowable only if the clause "Partial shipment to be allowed" is agreed upon in the sales contract. Or the clause "No partial shipment" should be given in the contract.

Transshipment in marine transportation is the movement of goods in transit from one carrier to another at the ports of transshipment before the goods reach the port of destination. Transshipment is necessary when ships going direct to the port of destination are not available, or the port of destination does not lie along the sailing route of the liner, or the amount of cargo for a certain port of destination is so small that no ships would like to call at that port. Transshipment is allowed when the sales contract has a clause like "transshipment to be allowed."

4. Shipping Documents

In marine transport, shipping document refers to marine transport bill of lading, shortened as B/L. B/L is issued by the captain or the shipping companies to testify that the goods have been received or shipped on board for delivery to a certain place of destination. It is an important marine transport shipping document that, together with the insurance policy and commercial invoices, constitutes the chief shipping documents indispensable to foreign trade.

There are several varieties of B/L, which are categorized in different ways:

(1) According to whether the goods have been shipped, bills of lading can be divided into on board B/L and received for shipment B/L.

The former is issued after the goods have been loaded on board, while the latter indicates the carrier has taken over the goods and prepared for shipment. In the trade contract, the buyer generally requires the seller to provide on board bill of lading.

(2) According to the apparent condition of the goods, that is whether there are negative comments on the B/L, bills of lading can be divided into clean B/L and unclean B/L.

The former means the shipment of the goods is in good condition. Clean B/L carries no unfavorable remarks by the carrier. The latter, unclean B/L carries such unfavorable remarks as "some packages appear in damaged condition," "iron strap loose or missing," "there are some breakage in packing," etc.

Normally, documentary credits require the clean B/L for negotiation. Any dirty or unclean B/L may be refused by the issuing bank and cause the seller great trouble.

(3) According to whether there is a specified name written in the column of consignee of the B/L, bills of lading can be divided into straight bill of lading (STRAIGHT B/L), and order bill of lading (ORDER B/L).

In Straight B/L, the name of the consignee is specified in the column of consignee. This means that the goods can only be received by the person specified and the B/L is not to be transferred to a third person. Therefore, a Straight B/L is not negotiable.

Order B/L does not have a specified name in the column of consignee of the B/L. In its place, usually there is only "to order," or "to the order of " — This means the consignee is designated according to the order of the shipper or the opening bank. It is called "made out to order." An Order B/L can be transferred to others by endorsement.

(4) According to different transport modes, bills of ladings can be divided into direct B/L, and transshipment B/L.

Under direct B/L, the consignment will directly be carried to the port of destination without transshipment, while under transshipment B/L, the consignment will be carried at least by two ships before it arrives at the port of destination. Generally, the buyer prefers a direct B/L because the possible cargo damage or losses may be caused by transshipment.

(5) According to the different forms, bills of ladings can be divided into long-form B/L and short-form B/L.

Long form B/L refers to the B/L with all the detailed terms and conditions about the rights and obligations of the carrier and the consignor listed on its back as an integrated part of the bill.

However, short-form B/L is a document which omits the terms and conditions on the back.

Part II Sample Letters

Sample 1 A Specimen of Bill of Lading

BILL OF LADING
CHINA OCEAN SHIPPING COMPAINY

Shipper_____   Head Office: Beijing
Consignee_____or Assigns   Branch Office: Guangzhou
                                                         Shanghai
                                                         Tianjin

Notify_____
                                          Cable Address: COSCO

BILL OF LADING
DIRECT OR WITH TRANSSHIPMENT

Vessel_____ Voy._____ S/O No. _____ B/L No. _____
Port of Loading_____   Port of Discharge_____
Nationality:_____   Freight Payable at_____

Particulars Furnished by the Shipper				
Marks and Number	No. of Packages	Description	Gross Wt.	Measurements

Total Packages (in words)	
Shipped on board the vessel named above in apparent good order and condition (unless otherwise indicated) the goods or packages specified herein and to be discharged at the above mentioned port of discharge or as near there to as the vessel may safely get and be always afloat. The weight, measurements, marks, numbers, quality, contents and value, being particulars furnished by the Shipper, are not checked by the Carrier on loading. The Shipper, Consignee and the Holder of this Bill of Lading hereby expressly accept and agree to all printed, written or stamped provisions, exceptions and conditions of this Bill of Lading, including those on the back hereof.	
Freight and Charges:	In witness whereof, the Carrier or his Agent has signed... Bills of Lading all of this tenor and date, one of which being accomplished, the others to stand void.
Shippers are requested to note particularly the exceptions and conditions of this Bill of Lading with reference to the validity of the insurance upon their goods.	Date____at _____for the Master

Sample 2 Shipping Instructions

Dear Sirs,

S/C No. 65p-2514

We acknowledge receipt of your letter dated the 4th this month enclosing the above sales contract in duplicate but wish to state that after going through the contract we find that the packing clause in it is not clear enough. The relative clause reads as follows:

Packing: Seaworthy export packing, suitable for long distance ocean transportation.

In order to eliminate possible future trouble, we would like to make clear beforehand our packing requirements as follows:

The tea under the captioned contract should be packed in international standard tea boxes 24 boxes on a pallet, 10 pallets in an FCL container. On the outer packing please mark our initials SCC in a diamond, under which the port of destination and our order number should be stenciled. In addition, warning marks like KEEP DRY, HANDLE WITH CARE should also be indicated.

We have made a footnote on the contract to that effect and are returning herein one copy of the contract after duly countersigning it. We hope you will find it in order and pay special attention to the packing.

We look forward to receiving your shipping advice and thank you in advance.

Yours faithfully,

Notes
1. packing clause 包装条款
2. seaworthy export packing 适合航海的出口包装
3. eliminate *v.* 排除
4. pallet *n.* 托盘，小货盘
5. FCL=Full Container Load 一整集装箱
6. to that effect 大意如此

部分常用的出口包装容器名称：

bag 袋，包	bale 包，布包	bundle 捆	barrel 琵琶桶
gunny bag 麻袋	polybag 塑料袋	box 盒，箱	carton 纸板箱
case 箱	wooden case 木箱	cask 木桶	crate 板条箱
drum 铁皮圆桶	keg 小圆捅	tin（英）=can（美）听，罐头	

Sample 3 Urging for Prompt Delivery

Dear Sirs,

Contract No. VW2563

We refer to the above contract signed between us on July 1, 2012 for 6,000 long tons of wheat, which is stipulated for shipment in October, 2012. However, up till now we have not received from you any information concerning the shipment of the goods.

As our end users are in urgent need of this material, we intend to send our vessel S.S. "Sian Hai" to pick up the goods, which is expected to arrive at Vancouver around the end of November. You are requested to let us have your immediate reply by fax whether you are agreeable to this proposal. If not, please let us know exactly the earliest time when the goods will be ready.

We have been put into great inconvenience by the delay in delivery. In case you should fail to effect delivery in November, we may be compelled to seek an alternative source of supply and lodge a claim against you for the loss. Please understand how serious and urgent it is and resolve this matter for us.

We look forward to receiving your shipping advice, by fax, within next week.

Yours faithfully,

Notes
1. pick up （车辆等）中途带（货）
2. lodge a claim against you for the loss 向你方提出损失索赔

Sample 4 Reply: Sending Shipping Advice

Dear Sirs,

Contract No. VW2563

Thank you very much for your letter of November 8 enquiring about the shipment of your order under Contract VW2563.

Please accept our apology for the delay in shipment of your goods which has been caused by no shipping space from London to your port.

The matter was, however, in hand and we are pleased to inform you that the 15,000 pieces of plush toy under your L/C No. MGM59 have been shipped on board S.S. "Wonderland" yesterday, which is scheduled to sail for your port on or about 12th November. Shipping details are as follows:

Contract No.:   VW2563
B/L No.:   BL0502681
Packing: 300 cartons
Voyage No.:   LZ1803

ETD:	Nov. 12, 2012
ETA:	Nov. 26, 2012
Container No.:	TEXU489235*1
Weight:	1,874kgs (N. W.)
	2,108kgs (G. W.)
Total Value:	US$ 38,469

Meanwhile we are enclosing the copies of shipping documents as follows:
    Commercial invoice No. KF-372 in duplicate
    Clean B/L No. BL0502681
    Packing List No. DK-201 in duplicate
    Insurance Policy No. AR18986
    Certificate of Quality
    Certificate of Quantity
    Survey Report No. FT2321

We trust the goods will reach you in time for the winter selling season and prove to be entirely satisfactory to you. I will personally ensure that you receive our prompt and careful attention all time.

Yours faithfully,

Notes
1. ETD: estimated time of departure 预计启程时间
2. ETA: estimated time of arrival 预计到达时间
3. commercial invoice 商业发票
4. packing list 装箱单
5. Bill of Lading 提单
6. insurance policy 保险单
7. survey report 检验报告

Sample 5   Booking Shipping Containers

Dear Sirs,

We have 100 cases of chemical reagents ready for dispatch to any EMP, and shall be glad if you will arrange for your shipping container to collect them. Each case weighs 60 kgs.

As our client requires us to ship the goods no later than July 15, please quote us for a shipping container from Qingdao to the above mentioned port before that deadline. Your early quotation will be highly appreciated.

Yours faithfully,

Notes
1. chemical reagents 化学试剂
2. EMP (European Main Ports) 欧洲主要口岸。按照航运公会统一规定，EMP 包括意大利的热那亚(Genoa)、法国的马赛 (Marseilles)、比利时的安特卫普(Antwerp)、荷兰的鹿特丹(Rotterdam)、英国的伦敦(London)、德国的汉堡 (Hamburg) 和丹麦的哥本哈根(Copenhagen)等港口。
3. shipping container 船运集装箱
   shipping mark 唛头
   shipping order 装货单，下货纸

Sample 6 Reply

Dear Sirs,

Thank you for your enquiry of June 5, asking us to quote for shipping containers to any EMP for 100 cases of chemical reagents.

The shipping containers we provide are of two sizes, namely 20 ft. and 40 ft. long and built to take loads up to 4 to 8 tons respectively. They can be opened at both ends, thus making it possible to load and unload at the same time. They are both watertight and airtight and can be loaded and locked at the factory, if necessary.

There is also a saving in freight charges when separate consignments intended for the same port of destination are carried in one container and an additional saving on insurance because of the lower premiums charged for container shipped goods.

We enclosed a copy of our tariff and look forward to receiving your instructions.

Yours faithfully,

Notes
1. watertight *adj.* 不漏水的，密封的
2. airtight *adj.* 不漏气的，密封的
3. freight *n.* 货物（特指装载于车船、飞机上的），运费
   freight charges 运费
   freight tariff 运费表
   freight rate 运费率
   freight service 货运
4. premium *n.* 保费
5. tariff *n.* 运费表，关税

Chapter Eight

Sample 7　The Change of the Modes of Transportation

Dear Sirs,
Re: Your L/C No.5757 covering your Order No.134

We learn from your shipping advice that the antique potteries and porcelain-ware we ordered on April 10 have been shipped by S.S. "Fengtao." According to the shipping schedule, it is expected to arrive in a day or two. However, after several contacts with the local forwarding agent, we are surprisingly told that the sail vessel has not yet arrived at Shanghai, let alone finished loading and set sail for Osaka. As the matter of fact, the goods are still lying at the dock in Shanghai waiting for shipment. These copies will not do you any good; on the contrary, they will prove deceptive manner in handling this transaction.

You may recall that we have time and again emphasized the vital importance of punctual shipment because these antique potteries and porcelain-ware are for display at an international exhibition to be held in Tokyo on July 9. We think it absurd to dispute with you over the delay in shipment on the present occasion when time is so pressing. The only remedy for avoiding non-performance of the contract we signed with the exhibition administration is to send the goods by air at once and at any cost. Please permit us to say that your cooperation in this regard is mandatory, for failure to have the antique potteries and porcelain put on display at the exhibition will not only cause us a heavy loss economically but also spoil your reputation and image as a famous porcelain manufacturer.

To be fair, we are prepared to pay for the airfreight, while you should be responsible for the other expenses such as shifting the goods from the dock to the airport.

We have instructed our bank to insert in the L/C the wording: "Shipment either by sea or by air" and are looking forward to receiving your confirmation that punctual arrival of the goods at Tokyo is guaranteed, i.e. on or about July 6.

Yours faithfully,

Notes
1. antique potteries 陶瓷古玩
2. porcelain-ware 瓷器
3. shipping schedule 装运日程安排
4. the forwarding agent 运输代理商
5. the only remedy for avoiding non-performance of the contract
    未履行合同的唯一补救措施
6. spoil your reputation and image 有损声誉和形象

Sample 8 Reply

Dear Sirs,

Your letter of May 21 has received our best attention. We apologize for the delay and also for the false information that the antique potteries and porcelain you ordered have been shipped by S.S. "Fengtao."

The said vessel is a tramp run by a foreign forwarding agency to sail the Pacific. In the past it did serve us to our satisfaction; for instance, a few shipments of glassware that required special care were handled in a way much better than expected. In light of such experience, we, therefore, entrusted "Fengtao" to effect the shipment. Unfortunately, it should have failed our expectation.

According to the forwarding agency, the duplicate copies of the B/L were sent by mistake as a result of confusion in work. They, in no way, implied any intention of deceiving the client. Nevertheless, we have cancelled the shipping space and firmly requested compensation for the losses we both have sustained.

Now the goods have been shifted to the airport waiting for dispatch to Tokyo tomorrow by Shanghai Airlines, Flight SHA-435. We believe this is the best solution of the case. All documents will be mailed by special express as soon as they are ready.

Yours sincerely,

Notes
1. tramp *n.* 不定期航船
2. in light of 鉴于
3. the losses we both have sustained 双方所蒙受的损失
4. by special express 用特快邮件

Part III Reading Materials

Moving Goods by Sea

The Different Types of Ocean Shipping

Many different types of ship are used to transport goods around the world. The differences between them reflect the varied needs of international traders. In particular, different types of ship are used to carry different types of cargo, or to carry cargo in varied ways.

The different types of ship are summarized below:

Chapter Eight

Container ships (or "box ships") carry their cargo packed into standard 20' or 40' containers that are stacked both on and below deck. Smaller "feeder" ships carry containers on coastal and inland waters.

Roll-on/roll-off (ro-ro) vessels[①] carry both road haulage and passenger vehicles.

General cargo ships carry loose, packaged cargo of all types.

Bulk carriers[②] carry unpackaged goods—usually large volumes of single-commodity goods such as grain, coal, fertilizers and ore.

Tankers[③] carry liquids (such as oil and gas) in bulk.

Merchant ships primarily do business in two different ways:

Liner vessels operate on fixed routes, to fixed schedules and usually with a standard tariff. Liner trades are dominated by container ships, roll-on/roll-off carriers and general cargo ships.

Charter ("tramp") vessels operate entirely according to the demands of the person chartering them. Their ports of loading and discharge are set by the charter, as is their cost, which depends on immediate supply and demand conditions. Most tankers and bulk carriers operate in the charter markets.

The Main International Shipping Routes

Shipping routes reflect world trade flows. Sailings are most numerous and most frequent on routes where trade volumes are the largest and demand is therefore the greatest.

In liner trades to and from the UK, the busiest routes are to the Far East (especially China and Japan), passing through the Mediterranean, the Suez Canal and the Malacca Straits[④]. The North Atlantic route, linking Western Europe and the USA and Canada, is also busy, and there are well-established routes to the Middle East, India, Australia and New Zealand, Central and South America, as well as to East and West Africa.

There are direct liner services from the UK to most other countries, and certainly to all the main trading economies. However, if your cargo is destined for a smaller port in one of these countries or for a port in a country with little trade with the UK, there may not be a direct sailing available—in which case, your cargo will need to be transshipped to another local sailing at the end of the ocean voyage.

In-bulk trade routes reflect the places of origin and consumption of the commodities carried. For example, many of the main oil routes begin in the Middle East and end in the developed countries where demand for oil is the greatest.

There will usually be a range of routes by which your cargo can reach its destination. It's worth exploring all the options available to find the one that best suits your needs in terms of price, speed, safety and contractual stipulations. This can be done by directly contacting those shipping companies that advertise sailings to your destination or by engaging freight forwarders to make arrangements for you.

The Costs of Ocean Shipping

There are two main elements to the cost of transporting goods by sea—the ocean freight charged by the carrier, and costs associated with handling and clearing the goods at the ports of loading and discharge.

A number of factors can influence how these charges are calculated:

For liner traffic, freight is usually charged according to the shipping company's standard tariff, although larger or frequent shippers and freight forwarders may be able to negotiate preferential shipping rates.

Charter rates for other vessels depend on supply and demand conditions prevailing at the time when the charter is negotiated.

However, there are many other factors that can impact on the final price, including:

Different rates for specific goods and general cargo:

Congestion charges at busy ports;

Currency adjustment factor, to take account of exchange rate changes during the journey—shipping costs are usually calculated and quoted in US dollars;

Bunker adjustment factor, to take account of fuel price fluctuation;

Surcharges (like a security surcharge) levied by ports and/or by the shipping company to cover the costs of particular regulatory regimes.

Another factor that affects the cost of shipping containerized cargo is whether or not you have a full container load to transport. Shipping companies' tariffs are based on flat per-container rates, so it is clearly most economical to ship your goods in containers that are full. If you have a less-than-container-load⑤ consignment, it may be worth consolidating your cargo with that of other traders, so you need only pay for the weight or volume (whichever is greater) of your own goods.

Working out the most cost-effective way to ship your goods around the world can be a complicated task. As with most services, you can research the options yourself or pay a third party (such as a freight forwarder) to handle these issues for you, finding transport modes and routes that suit your needs.

Notes

① roll-on/roll-off (ro-ro) vessels 滚装轮
② bulk carriers 散货船
③ tanker *n.* 邮轮
④ the Malacca Straits 马六甲海峡
⑤ less-than-container-load（LCL）拼箱货

Questions

1. What types of ships are used to carry different cargos?
2. What are the main international shipping routes?
3. What are the influential factors for the cost of transporting goods by sea?

Exercises

I. Fill in the blanks with the best choice:

1. We will do our best to _____ shipment to meet your requirements in due

Chapter Eight

course.
- a. comply
- b. make
- c. expedite
- d. deliver

2. The shipment time is April or May at our _____ and the goods will be shipped in one _____.
   - a. choice, shipment
   - b. option, lot
   - c. decision, cargo
   - d. opinion, consignment

3. We regret our inability to _____ with your request for shipping the goods in early December.
   - a. compliance
   - b. comply
   - c. manage
   - d. arrange

4. Before deciding which form of transport to use, a _____ will take into account the factors of cost, speed and safety.
   - a. consignor
   - b. consignee
   - c. shipper
   - d. ship owner

5. Since two-thirds of the voyage is in tropical weather and the goods are liable to go mouldy, we think it advisable to have the shipment _____ the risk of mould.
   - a. covered insurance
   - b. taken out insured
   - c. covered against
   - d. insured for

6. Before shipment, the buyers usually send their _____ to the sellers.
   - a. shipping advice
   - b. shipping instructions
   - c. shipping date
   - d. shipping port

7. The sellers usually send the _____ to the buyers immediately after the goods are loaded on board the ship, advising them of the shipment.
   - a. shipping advice
   - b. shipping instructions
   - c. shipping date
   - d. shipping port

8. Partial shipment may be necessary when _____.
   - a. direct liners are not available
   - b. the amount of the cargo is very small
   - c. the shipping date is very close.
   - d. the export covers a large amount of goods

9. If a B/L can be transferable, it is a _____.
   - a. clean B/L
   - b. transshipment B/L
   - c. order B/L
   - d. on board B/L

10. Based on whether the goods are loaded or not, the B/L can be classified into _____.
    - a. clean B/L and unclean B/L
    - b. direct B/L and transshipment B/L
    - c. straight B/L and order B/L
    - d. on board B/L and received for shipment B/L

11. For the goods under S/C No. 664, we _____ space on S.S. Dongfeng due to arriving in London around May 13.

    a. have booked   b. have bought
    c. have hired   d. have retained

12. The adoption of containers facilitated _____ to a great extent.
    a. to load and unload   b. the loading and unloading
    c. us to load and unload   d. loaded and unloaded

II. Translate the following sentences into English:

1. 只要你们能保证产品质量并且交货迅速，一定会得到我们的续订订单。
2. 兹通知你方，第678号销售合同项下货物已于7月5日装"南海"轮运出，在汉堡转船，预计9月初抵达你港。
3. 我们将按要求将清洁的已装船，空白抬头提单一式三份交由米德兰商业银行转交你方。
4. 我们女式上衣的包装为每件套一塑料袋，十打装一纸板箱，内衬防潮纸，外打铁箍两道。
5. 关于订单第689号下1000个计算器，我们希望提醒你们装运期已逾期很久。
6. 请说明你方报盘是否包括木箱包装费用。
7. 按合约所定，上述货物应在四月、六月和八月分三批等量装运，但直到现在第一批货还没有装。
8. 两万公吨大豆因舱位不够，无法提前全部在十月份装船，请修改信用证，允许分批装运。
9. 运到我们口岸的货物必须在汉堡转船，因此你们的包装必须具有适航性，并经得起运输途中的粗鲁搬运。
10. 非常高兴通知你方，我们已将你方订单145号货订好了"上海1号"的舱位，估计到达时间（ATA）是8月20日。

III. Translate the following sentences into Chinese:

1. We regret our inability to ship the goods in early November because the direct steamer sailing for your port calls at our port only on or after the 26th of November.
2. As the package of the goods was not strong enough to withstand the rough sea voyage, shipment was withheld at the last minute in order to give time for packaging improvement.
3. We wish to call your attention to the fact that we have not been advised by you of shipment of the order we booked last month.
4. If you agree to ship the goods in two equal lots, please let us know so that we can make arrangements accordingly.
5. We shall be very much obliged if you will effect shipment as soon as possible thus to enable our customer to catch the brisk demand at the start of the season.
6. According to the terms of Contract No.318, shipment is to be effected by the 20th Jan., and we must have the B/L by the 31st at the latest. We trust you will ship the order within the stipulated time as any delay would cause us no little inconvenience and financial loss.
7. We regret our inability to comply with your request for shipping the goods in early December, because the direct steamer sailing for London calls at our Port only around the 20th every month.

8. We are pleased to inform you that the goods under your Order No.1234 were shipped by the direct steamer "Red Star" on Nov.30, and the relevant shipping samples had been dispatched to you by air before the steamer sailed.
9. With regard to your Order No. 80 for 500 Sewing Machines, we shipped the goods by S.S. "East Wind" on 30th Nov. We trust that this shipment will arrive at your end shortly. Please let us have the comments of your end-users on the quality of our Sewing Machines.
10. In practice, shipment involves such procedures as clearing the goods through the customs, booking shipping space or chartering a ship, completing shipping documentation, dispatching shipping advice, etc.

IV. Letter writing:

Write a shipping advice to notify the buyer the shipping of 1,000 dozen men's shirts on board S.S. "Qingdao" sailing for the destination port on 15th November. Shipping documents include one copy of certificate of Quantity, one copy of Insurance Policy and Weight Memo in duplicate.

附录:

	B/L NO. COSU294831330
1. Shipper Insert Name, Address and Phone GUANGDONG NATIVE PRODUCE IMPORT & EXPORT CORPORATION (GROUP)	中远集装箱运输有限公司 COSCO CONTAINER LINES TLX: XXXX COSCO CN FAX: 86(20) XXXX XXXX **ORIGINAL**
2. Consignee Insert Name, Address and Phone TO ORDER	Port-to-Port or Combined Transport **BILL OF LADING**
3. Notify Party Insert Name, Address and Phone SUNRY IMPORT & EXPORT CO. LTD., LONDON FAX.0044-181-9606196, TEL.0044-181-9604805	RECEIVED — external apparent good order and condition except as otherwise noted. The total number of packages or units stuffed in the container, the description of the goods and the weights shown in this Bill of Lading are furnished by the Merchants, and which the carrier has no reasonable means of checking and is not a part of this Bill of Lading contract. The carrier has issued the number of Bills of Lading stated below; all of this same kind and date one of the original Bills of Lading must be surrendered and endorsed in exchange against the delivery of the shipment, and whereupon any other original Bills of Lading shall be void. The Merchants agree to be bound by the terms and conditions of this Bill of Lading as if each had personally signed this B/L of Lading. SEE clause 4 on the back of this Bill of Lading. Terms continued on the back hereof, please read carefully. * Applicable Only when Document Used as a Combined Transport Bill of Lading
4. Combined Transport* — CHENFER 513 V.0163M 6. Ocean Vessel/ Voy No. DA HE V.0057W 8. Port of Discharge BREMEN, GERMANY W/T HONG KONG	5. Combined Transport* Place of Receipt 7. Port of Loading HUANGPU 9. Combined Transport* Place of Delivery

Marks & Nos. Container Seal No	No. of Containers or Packages	Description of Goods (If Dangerous Goods, See Clause 20)	Gross Weight Kgs	Measurement
CGR WW 6873B-1104 N.W.225KGS BREMEN TTL:12X20'FCL CY/CY CNTR NO./SEAL NO. TEXU2192750/04265 CBHU0404920/001634 CBHU0584349/04264 MLCU2735066/001588 FBZU6120232/145782 FBZU0042791/04262	1104DRUMS CBHU0931690/04263 CBHU0864360/001635 FBZU3096960/145781 CBHU0927411/001767 CBHU3005266/04261 CBHU0130120/04269	SHIPPER'S LOAD & COUNT & SEAL S.T.C. GUM ROSIN FREIGHT PREPAID SHIPPED ON BOARD DATE:NOV.12,1998 VESSEL:CHENFER 513 V.0163M [seal: CHINA OCEAN SHIPPING AGENCY GUANGZHOU (8)]	256680KGS	309.120BM

Description of Contents for Shipper's Use Only (Not part of This B/L Contract)

10. Total Number of containers and/or packages in words. Subject to Clause 7 Limitation — TOTAL: ONE THOUSAND ONE HUNDRED AND FOUR DRUMS ONLY.

11. Freight & Charges	Revenue Tons	Rate	Per	Prepaid	Collect
Declared Value Charge					

AS AGENT FOR THE CARRIER:
COSCO CONTAINER LINES
SHIPPED ON BOARD
中国广州外轮代理公司

Ex. Rate	Prepaid at	Payable at	Place and date of issue GUANGZHOU NOV.12,1998
	Total Prepaid	Nor. of Original B(s)/L THREE/3	Signed for the Carrier, COSCO CONTAINER LINES C° INA OCEAN SHIPPING AGENCY GUANGZHOU AS AGENTS (8)

LADEN ON BOARD THE VESSEL
DATE   BY
(COSCON STANDARD FORM 9991)

CNG 98 0123241

中华人民共和国出入境检验检疫
ENTRY - EXIT INSPECTION AND QUARANTINE OF THE PEOPLE'S REPUBLIC OF CHINA

共1页第1页 Page 1 of 1
编号 No.: 321300207033287

品质证书
CERTIFICATE OF QUALITY

发货人 NANJING NEW STAR INTERNATIONAL TRADE CO., LTD.
Consigor 1505 ROOM, 15th FLOOR, NEWSPAPER BUILDING NO.233 LONGPANZHONG ROAD, NANJING, CHINA

收货人
Cconsignee

品名
Description of Goods   WHEAT FLOUR

标记及号码
Mark & No.

报检数量/重量
Quantity/Weight Declared   25200BAGS/630000KGS

包装种类及数量
Number and Type of Packages   25200PP BAGS

WINNER
WHEAT FLOUR
25KGS. NET. WT.
PRODUCED IN CHINA

运输工具
Means of Conveyance   BY VESSEL

As per GB5491-85, the representative samples drawn from the above goods were inspected against the S/C with the results as follows:
1. Sensory examination:
   Colour, taste & odour, appearance are normal;
   Free from foreign matters.
2. Physical & chemical analysis:
   Moisture: 12.9%;
   Ash: 0.54%;
   Wet Gluten: 32.6%;
   Protein: 11.8%.
Conclusion: The quality of the above mentioned goods is in conformity with the requirements of the S/C
****

签证地点 Place of Issue   ZHENJIANG   签证日期 Date of Issue   03 DEC., 2007

授权签字人 Authorized Officer   DING ZHICHENG   签 名 Signature

我们已尽所知和最大能力实施上述检验，不能因我们签发本证书面免除卖方或其他方面根据合同和法律所应承担的产品质量责任和其他责任。All inspections are carried out conscientiously to the best of our knowledge and ability. This certificate does not in any respect absolve the seller and other related parties from his contractual and legal obligations especially when product quality is concerned.

[(c1-1(2011.1.1)]

B 0422171

Chapter Nine

Insurance

Part I Introduction

1. Definition

Cargo transport insurance is to protect the interests of importers and exporters from possible financial losses caused by risks during the transit of goods from the factory or warehouse in a country of origin to the warehouse in a country of destination.

Originally, insurance was only applied to losses at the sea, where risks were always great. What's more, ocean shipping takes up the biggest share of the volume of goods transported in international trade. Therefore, marine insurance has become the most important insurance.

Marine insurance is defined as a contract of insurance whereby the insurer in return for premiums collected undertakes to indemnify the insured in a manner and to the extent thereby agreed, against marine losses, that is to say, the losses incidental to marine adventure. Such insurance involving the maritime conveyance of cargo from one country to another is, then, marine cargo insurance, which is seen as an indispensable adjunct to foreign trade.

2. Risks, Losses and Expenses

Different risks mean different losses, and different risks are covered by different insurance clauses and further different insurance clauses mean different premiums. Therefore, it is important to have a good understanding of the different risks and losses.

(1) Risks

Risks in marine cargo insurance are of many kinds, which can be classified into two types: perils of the sea and extraneous risks. Perils of the sea are caused by natural calamities and fortuitous accidents; the latter, by various extraneous reasons, including general extraneous risks and special extraneous risks.

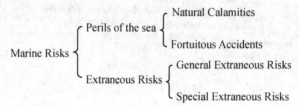

Natural calamity refers to the perils under force majeure such as vile weather, thunder storm and lightening, tsunami, earthquake, flood, etc.

Fortuitous accidents are such risks as ship stranding, striking upon the rocks, ship sinking, ship collision, colliding with icebergs or other objects, fire, explosion, ship missing, etc.

General extraneous risks include theft or pilferage, rain, shortage, contamination, leakage, breakage, taint of odor, dampness, heating, rusting, hooking, etc.

Special extraneous risks include war risks, strikes, non-delivery of cargo, refusal to receive cargo, etc.

(2) Losses

Marine losses are the damages or losses of the insured goods incurred by the above risks. The losses and damages done to the goods can fall into two types: total loss and partial loss. Total loss of goods can further be actual total loss and constructive total loss. Partial loss can be either general average or particular average.

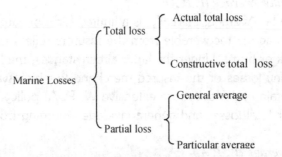

Actual total loss means the whole lot of the consignment has been lost or damaged or found valueless upon the arrival at the port of destination.

The constructive total loss is found in the case where the actual loss of the insured goods is unavoidable, or the cost to be incurred in recovering or reconditioning the goods together with the forwarding cost to the destination named in the policy would exceed their value on arrival.

In the insurance business the term "average" simply means "loss" in most cases. General average is in use when both the ship and the consignments on board are endangered and the captain, for the safety of the ship and the consignments on board, intentionally and reasonably does some sacrifices or makes some expenses.

A particular average loss means that a particular consignment is partially damaged.

(3) Expenses

Transportation insurance not only insures the losses caused by risks but also the losses of expenses. Expenses fall into the following kinds:

Sue and labour expenses

These expenses are the expenses arising from measures properly taken by the insured, the employee and the assignee, etc. for minimizing or avoiding losses caused by the risks covered in the insurance policy. The insurer is held responsible to compensate for such expenses.

Salvage charges

Salvage charges are expenses resulting from measures properly taken by a third party other than the insured, the employee and the assignee, etc.

Continuation expenses

Continuation expenses are made for continuing the journey of consignments after the journey has been stopped by risks under the cover of the insurance policy.

Loss evaluation charges

After a loss is sustained, experts would have to be invited to evaluate the loss to be covered by the insurer. These expenses are usually covered by the insurer.

3. Marine Insurance Coverage

Under China Insurance Clause (C.I.C.), for ocean marine insurance, there are basic risks coverage and additional risks coverage. Basic risks coverage falls into three groups: Free from Particular Average (F.P.A), With Particular Average (W.P.A) and All Risks. Additional risks include general additional risks and special additional risks.

(1) Basic risks coverage

Free From Particular Average (F. P. A)

Free from Particular Average, basically, is a limited form of cargo insurance in that no partial loss or damage is recoverable from the insurers unless that actual vessel or craft is stranded, sunk or burnt. Under the latter circumstances, the F.P.A. cargo policy holder can recover any losses of the insured merchandise which was on the vessel at the time as would obtain under the more extensive W. P. A. policy. The F.P.A. policy provides coverage for total losses and general average emerging from actual "marine perils".

With Particular Average (W. P. A.)

With Particular Average covers wider than F. P. A. Aside from the risks covered under F. P. A., this insurance also covers partial losses of the insured goods caused by vile weather, lightning, tsunami, earthquake and/or flood.

All Risks

The cover of All Risks is the most comprehensive of the three. Aside from the risks covered under F. P. A. and W. P. A. conditions, this insurance also covers all risks of loss or damage to the insured goods whether partial or total, arising from external causes in the course of transit. It should be noted that "All Risks" does not, as its name suggests, really cover all risks. The "All Risks" clause excludes coverage against damage caused by war, strikes, riots, etc. These perils can be covered by separate clause. And All Risks covers only physical loss or damage from external causes.

(2) Additional Insurance Coverage

According to the nature of the goods insured, the cargo owner may choose any of the three basic covers mentioned above. If more protections are needed, he may further insure his goods against one or several additional risks. No additional risk can be purchased to insure goods independently.

General Additional Risks

General Additional Risks include:
- Theft, pilferage and non-delivery risk
- Fresh water and/or rain damage risk
- Shortage risk
- Intermixture and contamination risk

- Leakage risk
- Clash and breakage risk
- Taint or odor risk
- Sweat and heating risk
- Hook damage risk
- Breakage of packing risk
- Rust risk

Special Additional Risks

Special Additional Risks include:
- War risk
- Strike risk
- On deck risk
- Import duty risk
- Rejection
- Aflatoxin
- Failure to deliver
- Fire Risk Extension Clause

4. Insurance Documents

Insurance documents are ones, issued by the insurer, certifying that the insurer and the insured have signed an insurance contract covering the goods to be transported. If the goods under the contract do incur damages or even losses in transit, the insured can lodge a claim against the insurance documents.

Since insurance documents are the evidence of insurance contract between the insurer and the insured, they are mainly classified as insurance policy, insurance certificate, cover note, etc.

(1) Insurance Policy

An insurance policy is a written legal contract between the insurer and the insured containing all terms and conditions of the agreement (normally pre-printed on the back of the policy). It shows full details of the risks covered, and is also called formal insurance documents.

Key elements of insurance policy are illustrated as follows:
- Name of the insurer with a signature identified as that of insurance company, or underwriter, or insurance agent.
- Name of the insured—both the seller and the buyer might be the insured if they have insured interest and with good faith.
- The insured goods with included description of subject matter.
- Type of risks covered—one of the three basic risks, i.e. F.P.A, W.P.A, and All Risks under CIC or ICC A, ICC B, and ICC C under ICC.
- Insurance provisions.
- Amount and currency insured.
- Place of claim payable.
- Transport model and vessel's name.
- Port of shipment and port of destination. If transshipment is required, the

goods should cover transshipment risks such as warehouse to warehouse clause including transshipment risks.
- Time and place of insurance.

(2) Insurance Certificate

An insurance certificate is a document issued to the insured certifying that the insurance has been effected. It contains the same details as an insurance policy except that version of provisions is abbreviated. If a documentary credit requires an insurance policy, the issuing bank will refuse an insurance certificate for payment.

Part II Sample Letters

Sample 1 A Specimen of Insurance Policy

中国人民保险公司
THE PEOPLE'S INSURANCE COMPANY OF CHINA
总公司设于北京　　一九四九年创立
Head Office: BEIJING　　Established in 1949

保险单
INSURANCE POLICY

发票号码　　　　　　　　　　　　　　　　保险单号次
Invoice No. NW081　　　　　　　　　　　Policy No. 2007PC773245

中国人民保险公司（以下简称本公司），根据上海新龙有限公司（以下简称被保险人）的要求，由被保险人向本公司缴付约定的保险费，按照本保险单承保险别和背面所载条款与下列特款承保下述货物运输，特立本保险单。

This Policy of Insurance witnesses that the People's Insurance Company of China (hereinafter called "the Company"), at the request of <u>SHANGHAI NEW DRAGON CO. LTD.</u> (hereinafter called "the Insured") and in consideration of the agreed premium being paid to the Company by the Insured; undertake to insure the undermentioned goods in transportation subject to the conditions of this Policy as per the Clause printed overleaf and other special clauses attached hereon.

标记 Marks & Nos.	包装及数量 Quantity	保险货物项目 Description of Goods	保险金额 Amount Insured
SUPERB **H.K.** **NO.1-75** **MADE IN CHINA**	75 CARTONS	80%COTTON 20% POLYESTER LADIES KNIT JACKET	USD28215.00

总保险金额：
　　　　Total Amount Insured <u>SAY U.S.DOLLARS TWENTY EIGHT THOUSAND TWO
　　　　　　　　　　HUNDRED AND FIFTEEN ONLY.</u>

保费　　　　　　　　费率　　　　　　　　装载运输工具
Premium as <u>arranged</u>　　Rate <u>as arranged</u>　　Per conveyance S.S <u>DONGFENG V. 229</u>
开航日期　　　　　　　　　　自　　　　　　　　　至
Slg. on or abt. <u>DEC. 12, 2007</u>　　From <u>SHANGHAI</u>　　　To <u>HONGKONG</u>
承保险别
Conditions <u>ALL RISKS AND WAR RISK AS PER CHINA INSURANCE CLAUSES.</u>
所保货物，如遇出险，本公司凭本保险单及其他有关证件给付赔款。

Chapter Nine

Claims, if any, payable on surrender of this Policy together with other relevant documents.
所保货物，如发生本保险单项下负责赔偿的损失或事故，应立即通知本公司下述代理人查勘。
In the event of accident whereby loss or damage may result in a claim under this Policy immediate notice applying for survey must be given to the Company's Agent as mentioned hereunder:

中国人民保险公司
THE PEOPLE'S INSURANCE COMPANY OF CHINA HONGKONG BRANCH
6-7F, SULAN BUILDING, CENTRAL HONG KONG

赔款偿付地点
Claim payable at DESTINATION IN THE CURRENCY OF THE DRAFTS.
日期
DATE: DEC. 5, 2007

中国人民保险公司
THE PEOPLE'S INSURANCE CO. OF CHINA

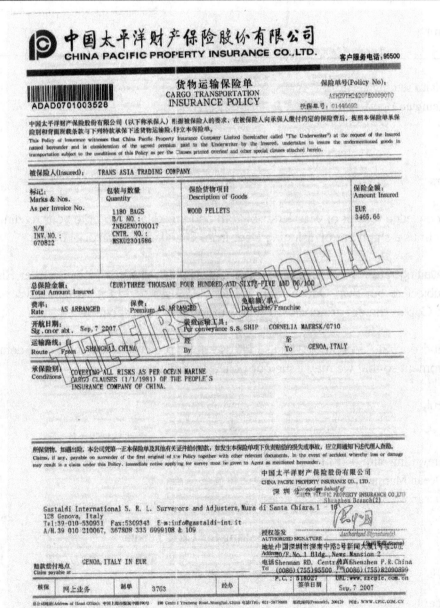

Sample 2 Application for Insurance

Dear Sirs,

Knowing that your company is the largest insurance company in China with branches and sub-branches throughout the country and survey and claim settling agents in major ports of the world, we, Tsingtao Brewery Co. Ltd., wish to insure with your company a shipment of Qingdao Beer valued at US $455,000 on board the vessel Hongyuan against All Risks, bound from Qingdao to Liverpool sailing on 20th March.

We shall appreciate it if the goods could be insured at a favorable rate.

Yours truly,

Note
1. claim settling agent 理赔代理
2. Tsingtao Brewery Co. Ltd. 青岛啤酒股份有限公司

Sample 3 The Reply

Dear Sirs,

We acknowledge receipt of your letter of 20th and are pleased to note your readiness to insure with us a shipment of Tsingtao Beer from Qingdao to Liverpool by sea.

The prevailing rate for the proposed shipment against All Risks including War Risks is 0.5%, subject to our own Ocean Marine Cargo Clauses and Ocean Marine War Risks Clauses. Copies thereof are enclosed herewith for your reference.

If you find our rate acceptable, please let us know, preferably, by cable, the details of your shipment so that we may issue our policy accordingly.

Yours truly,

Notes
1. prevailing rate 现行汇率，市价
2. Ocean Marine Cargo Clauses 海洋运输货物保险条款
3. Ocean Marine War Risks Clauses 海洋运输货物战争险条款

Sample 4 Asking for CFR Terms

Dear Sirs,

Insurance

We thank you for your letter of May 10, quoting us 100 metric tons of Wool on CIF terms. We regret, however, that we prefer to have your quotations and/or offers on CFR terms.

For your information, we have taken out an open policy with the Lloyd Insurance Company, London. All we have to do when a shipment is made is to advise them of the particulars. Furthermore, we are on very good terms with them. We usually receive from our underwriters quite a handsome premium rebate at regular intervals.

In the meantime, we should appreciate it if you could supply us with full details regarding the scope of cover handled by the People's Insurance Company of China for our reference.

We look forward to hearing further from you at an early date.

Yours faithfully,

Notes
1. insurance *n.* 保险
    insurance certificate 保险凭证
    insurance coverage 保险范围
    insurance premium 保（险）费
    to cover insurance 投保，洽办保险
2. insure *v.* 保险，投保
    Please insure the goods against All Risks and War Risk.
    请为货物投一切险和战争险。
    Please insure against Breakage.
    请投破损险。
3. take out 通过申请而取得；办理（保险）手续
4. Lloyd Insurance Company, London 伦敦劳埃德保险公司
5. on good terms with sb. 与某人关系良好
6. underwriter *n.* 保险商
7. rebate *n.* 回扣
8. cover *n.* 保险，投保
    We have arranged the necessary insurance cover.
    我们已经办理了必要保险。
    cover *v.* 保险，投保
    We shall cover the goods against All Risks.
    我们将为货物投一切险。

Sample 5 Importer Asks Exporter to Cover Insurance

Dear Sirs,

Re: Our Order No. 101
　　Your S/C No. 013

Covering 500 cases of Electronic Toys

We wish to refer you to our Order No. 101 for 500 cases Electronic Toys, from which you will see that this order was placed on CFR basis.

As we now desire to have the consignment insured at your end, we shall be much pleased if you will kindly arrange to insure the same on our behalf against All Risks for 110% of the invoice value.

We shall, of course refund the premium to you upon receipt of your debit note or, if you like, you may draw on us at sight for the same.

We sincerely hope that our request will meet with your approval.

Yours faithfully,

Notes
　1. consignment *n.* （货物）交货，发货，货物，寄存物
　2. refund *v.* 退还，偿还
　　　　　n. 偿还额，退款
　　　refund the premium 退还保金
　3. debit note 借方通知，借方账单，即欠账单

Sample 6 Insurance Company Asks to Cancel Breakage Risk

Dear Sirs,

Additional Risk of Breakage

We refer to your L/C No. 157 covering Glazed Wall Tiles, which we have just received.

Please note for this article we do not cover Breakage. You have to, therefore, delete the word "Breakage" from the insurance clause in the credit.

Furthermore, we wish to point out that for such articles as window glass, porcelains, etc., even if additional Risk of Breakage has been insured, the cover is subject to a franchise of 5%. In other words, if the breakage is surveyed to be less than 5%, no claims for damage will be entertained.

We trust that the position is now clear. Please fax the amendment immediately.

Yours faithfully,

Notes
1. glazed wall tile 釉面墙砖
2. porcelain *n.* 瓷器,瓷
3. franchise *n.* 免赔率(额);特权,特许
4. No claims for damage will be entertained.
   将不予考虑对损失的索赔。

Sample 7 A Reply to the Request for Excessive Insurance

Dear Sirs,

Your Order No. 523 for 5,000 pcs. Gunny Bags

We have received your fax of January 23, asking us to insure the captioned order for an amount of 30% above the invoice value.

Although it is our usual practice to insure shipments for the invoice value plus 10%, we are prepared to comply with your request for getting cover for 130% of the invoice value. But the extra premium will be for your account.

We trust the above will be acceptable to you.

Yours faithfully,

Notes
1. excessive insurance 超额投保
2. an amount of 30% above the invoice value 发票金额加价30%
3. But the extra premium will be for your account.
   额外保费由你方负担。

Sample 8 Insurance Claim

Dear Sirs,

When the S.S. "Eancastria" arrived at Tripoli on 10th November, it was noticed that one side of the Case No. 9 containing MP5 was split. We, therefore, had the case opened and the content examined by a local insurance surveyor in the presence of the shipping company's agents. The case was invoiced as containing twenty-four "Star" MP5s, six of which were badly damaged.

We enclosed the surveyor's report and the shipping agent's statement. As our order was placed on CIF basis and you covered the insurance, we should be grateful if you would take the matter up for us with the insurers. Six replacement MP5s will be required. Please arrange the replacement on our account.

We hope no difficulty will arise in connection with the insurance claim and thank you in advance for your cooperation.

Yours faithfully,

Notes
1. Tripoli 的黎波里
2. a local insurance surveyor 当地保险公司货物检验员
3. The case was invoiced as containing twenty-four "Star" MP5s, six of which were badly damaged.
该箱发票明细为24个"星"牌MP5，其中6个破损严重。

Part III   Reading Materials

Passage One

The Cost of Calamity

The economic impact of natural disasters is often short-lived. Will this be the case in Japan?

The full extent of the damage from the tsunami that hit Japan's north-eastern coast on March 11, 2011 is not yet known, but early estimates of the cost are big. Rebuilding homes, factories, roads and bridges could cost as much as US$200 billion, some reckon. Quite apart from these direct costs, is the disaster likely to do lasting harm to Japan's economy?

Much will depend on the success of efforts to prevent a nuclear catastrophe[①]. Assuming the situation at the Fukushima Dai-ichi plant[②] stabilizes, the contours of the economic impact of the tsunami itself can already be discerned. Natural disasters disrupt production, much as less destructive episodes of bad weather[③] do. In Japan the interruption to electricity supply means that output has been affected even in areas the tsunami did not directly inundate. Toyota, for example, halted production because of problems with parts and supplies. Operations were suspended in six of Sony's factories, only one of which was flooded.

But such disruption is unlikely to persist. On March 16 Toyota announced that it was restarting the production of spare parts. As with bad weather, disasters cause some output to be postponed rather than lost. When production résumés, it is likely to be at a faster clip than usual. Studies of the economic effects of past natural disasters, as well as Japan's own experience after the 1995 earthquake in Kobe[④], provide further reassurance. They suggest that the macroeconomic effects of the tsunami, though hardly negligible, will not be devastating and will not last very long.

How much a natural disaster reduces output over the medium term[⑤] depends on a number of factors. Location matters: disasters that strike an industrial belt will be more economically crippling than ones that hit an area where little is produced; the economic effects of the tsunami would have been much worse if it had struck Japan's industrial heartland. And different kinds of natural disasters have different consequences for growth. In the medium term, not all effects are negative. A 2009 World Bank study found that by increasing soil fertility, a typical flood increases agricultural output in the year after it strikes (though output falls in the year it occurs). The benefits from higher agricultural production spill over to other sectors, and in developing countries where the farm sector is a bigger part of the economy, this may be enough to lead to faster growth in manufacturing and services in subsequent years.

Earthquakes, on the other hand, have small but consistently negative effects on economic growth. This is because earthquakes do not just shut production down for a while. They also destroy factories, roads, electricity lines and offices. This destruction does not directly reduce a country's GDP, which measures the value of the flow of goods and services that an economy produces. But it does affect an economy's underlying productive capacity. The Japanese tsunami fits this template.

As long as these assets remain out of commission, the output they would have produced is, in theory, lost. In practice, this negative effect can partly be made up by using plant and machinery in areas unaffected by the disaster. Most factories do not run at full steam all the time; output from plants that are still working can be increased to make up for lost production elsewhere.

An analysis of the effect of the Kobe earthquake by George Horwich of Purdue University[⑥] provides some reason to hope that this might happen in Japan. The quake ravaged many of the facilities of what were then the world's sixth-largest container port and the source of nearly 40% of Kobe's industrial output. Over 100,000 buildings were completely destroyed, and many more badly damaged; 300,000 people were rendered homeless; over 6,000 died. Yet despite this devastation in a big production centre, the local economy recovered very fast. Even though less than half the port facilities had been rebuilt by that stage, within a year import volumes through the port had recovered fully and export volumes were nearly back to where they would have been without the disaster. Less than 15 months after the earthquake, in March 1996, manufacturing activity in greater Kobe was at 98% of its projected pre-quake level.

Mr. Horwich reckons that the likely reason for this rebound in output and economic activity, even as swathes of infrastructure still lay in ruins[⑦], is that output can be produced using different combinations of labor and capital. Although a disaster may destroy physical capital, things can be made using more labor or using it more intensively than before. In addition, rebuilding is easier than building up capital the first time around, because it mainly aims to replicate a pattern of investment rather than figure out what to invest in. And productivity growth may accelerate when new, and often superior, machinery is installed.

Reconstruction itself, of course, also helps to offset the negative impact of a drop in output in the aftermath of a disaster. Business booms for builders and producers of capital goods. Disasters probably do not actually stimulate the economy because additional production in some sectors may be displacing spending elsewhere, though this is less of a worry in an economy with a lot of spare capacity⑧. Certainly, the year of the Kobe quake was not a bad one for the Japanese economy, which grew by 1.9% in 1995 compared with 0.9% growth in 1994.

There are grounds to hope, then, that this month's terrible events will not cause lasting damage to Japan's economy. But there are worries, too. The nuclear crisis adds greatly to uncertainty. Consumer and business confidence is fragile. With interest rates already at zero, policymakers have little wiggle room⑨. Japan's manufacturing sector is running closer to full capacity now than in the mid-1990s, making it harder to make up for lost output. Whenever disasters occur, for most of the cases, they will do lasting harm to a nation's economy.

Notes

① a nuclear catastrophe 核灾难
② the Fukushima Dai-ichi plant 福岛一号核反应堆
③ destructive episodes of bad weather 天灾
④ earthquake in Kobe 坂神大地震
⑤ over the medium term 从中期来看
⑥ Purdue University 普渡大学
⑦ even as swathes of infrastructure still lay in ruins 即使基础设施满目苍夷尚未恢复
⑧ spare capacity 闲置产能
⑨ have little wiggle room 几乎没有回旋的余地

Questions

1. What do you think about the consequence of natural calamities?
2. Why do earthquakes usually have consistently negative effects on economy growth?

Exercise

I. Fill in the blanks with the best choice:

1. We shall cover the shipment _____ 10% above the invoice value.
   a. at   b. with
   c. for   d. by
2. If you desire us to insure _____ a special risk, an extra premium will be charged.
   a. against   b. for
   c. with   d. on
3. Buyer's request for insurance to be covered up to the inland city can be

accepted on condition that such extra premium is for _____ account.
   a. the seller's   b. the buyer's
   c. the insurer's   d. the insured's
4. We wish to point out that for porcelains the cover is subject to a _____ of 5%.
   a. insurance   b. franchise
   c. premium   d. coverage
5. We have covered insurance _____ the 500 sets of sewing machines.
   a. on   b. with
   c. about   d. by
6. In marine transportation, risks fall into two types, namely, _____.
   a. natural calamities and fortuitous accidents
   b. perils of the sea and extraneous risks
   c. general average and particular average
   d. general risks and special risks
7. The losses and damages done to the goods in marine transportation can be classified into two types, namely _____.
   a. actual total loss and constructive total loss
   b. general average and particular average
   c. basic loss and additional loss
   d. total loss and partial loss
8. We have _____ an open policy with the People's Insurance Company of China.
   a. made out   b. set out
   c. taken out   d. carried out
9. Please kindly arrange insurance on our behalf against All Risks and we shall, of course, refund the _____ to you.
   a. insurance   b. franchise
   c. premium   d. coverage
10. As per our contract, insurance shall be _____ by the buyer.
    a. effected   b. taken
    c. amended   d. drawn

II. Translate the following sentences into English:
1. 现欣然奉告，第564号合同项下10,000吨化肥即装"青山"轮，该轮定于5月25日起航，请为此货办理保险事宜。
2. 请注意（做到），保险须按发票金额的110%投保一切险和战争险。
3. 我们知道按照你方惯例，你们只按发票金额加价10%投保，因此，额外保费由我方负担。
4. 若我方客户没有具体要求，我们通常投保水渍险和战争险。如果你方想要投保平安险，请事先告知。
5. 破碎险的保费率是2%，如果你方愿意投保破碎险，我方可以代为办理，但额外保费由你方负担。
6. 此货需保渗漏险。
7. 我们将对你方订货投保偷窃、提货不着险。

8. 此类商品按免赔率4%出售。
9. "一切费用由受益人负担"之条款应从信用证中删除。
10. 由于水泥在运输途中非常易于受潮或受雨淋而变质,因此务必采取必要的防护措施使得包装能够防潮和免遭雨水侵蚀。

III. Translate the following sentences into Chinese:

1. Insurance on the goods shall be covered by us for 110% of the CIF value, and any extra premium for additional coverage, if required, shall be borne by the buyers.
2. The insurance company insures this risk with 5% franchise.
3. Should any damage occur, you may put in a claim with the insurance company within 60 days after the arrival of the consignment.
4. We wish to reiterate that it is only in view of our long friendly business relations that we extend you this accommodation.
5. Please find enclosed our invoice for HK$ 100,000 and note that we have drawn on you for this amount at 30 days attaching the shipping documents to our draft.
6. In case that you have any specific requirements for the insured amount or insurance coverage, please let us know and we will do our utmost to be of service to you.
7. The difference between CIF and CFR prices depends on the nature of the goods to be insured, the degree of coverage desired and the place of destination.
8. We leave the insurance arrangement to you, but we wish to have the goods covered against All Risks.
9. We would like to remind you of insuring the above shipment under Contract No. 2112 in due course.
10. We are pleased to confirm having insured the above shipment for 130% of the invoice value with the agent of the PICC against All Risks for US$ 2,200.

IV. Letter writing:

Write a letter to ask for additional insurance (broader coverage) over the usual FPA, on 100,000 M/T of chemical fertilizer and make it clear which party is responsible for the extra premium (make your own assumptions as to other conditions).

Chapter Ten

Complaints and Claims

Part I Introduction

1. Claims and Complaints

On execution of a sales contract, both parties to the contract must strictly perform their respective obligations. If one of the parties breaches the contract, the other may run into trouble, or suffer great losses. In this case, the affected party is entitled to request the defaulter to make up his losses according to the relevant provisions under the contract. Such request the affected party makes for compensation is called "claim": that the party responsible for the losses or damage takes measures to deal with the claim one way or another is called "settlement of claim."

Claim is a common occurrence in foreign trade practice, but it does not mean that it will happen in every transaction. However, the affected party, in consideration of the good relation with the other party, or the loss incurred being a minor one, sometimes does not lodge a claim against the suppliers, but rather requests him to make sure that such things will not happen again. This is known as a "complaint" rather than a claim.

2. Cases Leading to Complaints and Claims

In international sales transaction, most claims are filed by buyer against seller such as the seller's failure to deliver the goods, late delivery or shipment of the goods, short weight, the goods' inconformity with the contract stipulation (including "shipping the inferior for the contracted quality goods"), incomplete documentation and damages caused by improper packing, etc.

However, there are times when the seller files claims against the buyer. This may occur when the buyer refuses or delays opening an L/C, delays sending a vessel to carry the goods under FOB terms or refuses to take delivery of the goods and so on.

3. Tips in Handling Claims

Generally speaking, the parties involved in a claim will first try to settle a claim through friendly negotiation, and avoid arbitration or litigation. We must keep the following points in mind when drafting a letter for handling a claim:

● Prompt in action

Generally all sales contracts stipulate a period for either party to file a claim, then that party must do it within the time limit. The party responsible for the claim should take immediate action to make investigations, send prompt reply to the affected party, and solve the problem in accordance with the international trade usages or conventions.

- Clear and complete in description

In a letter of claim, the affected party should give a clear description of the loss or damage he has incurred, and also state the reason why the addressee should be responsible for the loss or damage. It is more convincing if the affected party can provide the relevant evidences, a certificate of inspection for example, to support his claim or request.

- Amicable in tone

Despite that dealing with a claim is no pleasant matter, we should be calm and reasonable in attitude when negotiating for a settlement. In a letter of claim, we must state our firm stand, but at the same time, should remain courteous, even when argumentation is inevitable. Being rude and emotional does not help to resolve a contradiction.

- Accurate in quotation

Sometimes we have to cite some instances as evidence to support our proposition based on the sales contract or business correspondence. Normally each letter, fax or email, has its date or reference number. We must make sure what we are going to quote from relevant letters, faxes or whatsoever and avoid getting them mixed up; otherwise, we would be put in an awkward position.

4. Settlement of Claims

In some sales contracts, the two parties often stipulate clauses on settlement of claims as well as inspection and claim causes.

In case the seller is liable for the nonconformity of the goods with the contract and a claim is made by the buyer within the period of claim or the period of quality guarantees stipulated in the sales contract, the seller may settle the claim upon the agreement of the buyer in the following ways.

- Agree to the rejection of the goods and refund to the buyer the value of the rejected goods in the same currency as contracted herein, and bear all direct losses and expenses incurred from the rejection, including interest, banking charges, freight, insurance premium, inspection charges, storage charges and all other necessary expenses required for the custody and protection of the rejected goods.

- Devaluate the goods according to the degree of inferiority, extent of damage and amount of losses suffered by the buyer.

- Replace the defective goods with new ones which conform to the specification, quality and performance as stipulated in the sales contract, and bear all expense incurred and direct losses sustained by the buyer. The seller shall, at the same time, guarantee the quality of the replaced goods for a further agreed period.

Chapter Ten

Part II Sample Letters

Sample 1 Claim for Improper Packing

Dear Sirs,

Our Order No. C568

We received this morning 20 cartons of Wool Carpet under our Order No. C568 per S.S. "CHANGFU." We found that one side of 8 cartons were worn and torn and 4 cartons were broken and the carpets were in the open. It was obviously attributed to improper packing.

Though the carpets can be used, we have to sell them at a price much lower than usual. In view of the above we suggest you give us 20% discount on the invoice value or we will have to return the goods to you and ask for replacements.

Please let us know your decision as soon as possible.

Sincerely yours,

Notes
1. worn and torn 磨损
2. It was obviously attributed to improper packing.
   显然是由于包装不当所致。

Sample 2 Reply

Dear Sirs,

We regret to learn from your letter of September 8 that your order of No. C568 of 20 cartons of Wool Carpet arrived in poor condition.

If it were our fault, we should be very glad to replace the damaged goods. However, in view of the fact that our goods were carefully packed by experienced workmen and sent out in perfect condition as is shown by a copy of the clean B/L which we hold, we are certain that they must have been damaged through careless handling during transit, or possibly been left out in the open and rained upon.

We, therefore, suggest that you enter a claim immediately against the shipping company. If you send us the papers which show exactly the condition in which the shipment reached you, we will take up the matter for you with a view to recovering damages from the shipping company.

We await your early reply.

Yours faithfully,

Notes
    1. in perfect condition 状况良好
    2. take up the matter 着手处理
    3. with a view to doing sth. 考虑做……

Sample 3 A Complaint for Inferior Quality

Dear Sirs,

It is with great regret that we have to inform you that your last delivery is not up to your usual standard. The material seems to be too loosely woven and is inclined to pull out of shape. By separate mail we have sent you a cutting from this material, also one from cloth of an early consignment, so that you can compare the two and see the difference in texture.

We have always been able to rely on the high quality of the materials you sent us and we are all the more disappointed in this case because we supplied the cloth to new customers. As we shall have to take it back, we must ask you to let us know, without delay, what you can do to help us in getting over this difficulty.

We wait for your early reply.

Sincerely yours,

Notes
    1. pull out of shape 走形
    2. texture *n.* 质地
    3. get over 克服，解决

Sample 4 The Seller Agrees to Settle the Claim

Dear Sirs,

We have received your letter of 14th October and thank you for sending us the two samples of cloth for examination.

We have passed these on to the manufacturer for comment and we quote the following from their reply:

"It was found that some short-staple yarn had, by mischance, been woven into the material and this cloth was put on one side for disposal in a suitable market. Evidently through an oversight some of the cloth was packed in your consignment. The factory manager was very grateful for the sample, as it is possible other buyers may have also received these imperfect goods, and enquiries are being made accordingly."

We told the manufacturers how greatly concerned we were over your disappointment in the quality, and the fact that you had supplied the cloth to new customers. They expressed their very great regret, and we have arranged with them for the immediate dispatch of replacements, Franco Domicile, Duty Paid. Furthermore, they guarantee the quality of the cloth now sent.

If you care to dispose of the inferior cloth at the best price obtainable for it, we will send you a Credit Note for the difference as soon as we hear from you.

We apologize sincerely for the trouble caused to you, and will take all possible steps to ensure that such a mistake is not made again.

Yours faithfully,

Notes
1. short-staple yarn 短纤维纱线
2. by mischance 疏忽，不留意
3. oversight *n*. 粗心，不留神
4. Franco Domicile, Duty Paid 相当于 INCONTERM 1990 中的 DDP，即 Delivered, Delivered, Duty Paid。该贸易条件意为卖方将货物运至进口国的指定地点来履行其交货义务。
5. Credit Note 付款（贷记）通知书

Sample 5 A Complaint of Short Delivery

Dear Sirs,

Information has just been received from Messrs. Bombey & Sons in Colombo, the consignees under B/L No. 20 dated February 25, that two of the 100 cases shipped from Huangpu to Colombo per S.S. "Baltrover" are missing.

The consignees contacted your agents in Colombo about it, and they were advised to get in touch with us direct to inquire into the matter.

As matters stand, it is legibly indicated in the B/L which is CLEAN and without qualification, that the 100 cases were shipped in apparent good order and condition. The same indication appears in our Shipping Order and your Mate's Receipt. It is, therefore, obvious that the shortage is due to your fault and we hereby notify you that we reserve the right to claim on you for the shortage, should it be subsequently confirmed.

Your early clarification and settlement of the case will be appreciated.

Sincerely yours,

Notes
1. as matters stand 事实是……, 照目前的情况
2. legibly *adv.* 字迹清楚地
3. qualification *n.* 限制条件, 限制
4. without qualification 无保留地
5. Mate's Receipt 大副收据, 收货单

Sample 6 An Adjustment Made by the Shipping Company

Dear Sirs,

Thank you for your letter of March 11. We have today received information from our agents in Karachi that the two cases referred to were over-carried and landed at that port. We are making immediate arrangements to have the goods returned to Colombo by the first opportunity available, and have instructed our agents there to notify your consignees of the returned parcel and bear any charges and expenses thus incurred for our account.

The matter stands thus that S.S. "Baltrover" departed from Colombo several hours ahead of schedule to tide over the ebbing. Our tallymen hurriedly covered the hatchways under the supervision of the customs officer, leaving the stowage intact. However, had the two cases not been stowed away from the bulk, we could have delivered the consignment in full.

Please accept our sincere apologies for the delay in delivery and the trouble which may have been caused to both the consignees and yourselves.

We assure you of our best services at all times.

Yours faithfully,

Notes
1. over-carry *v.* 越载

2. bear any charges and expenses thus incurred for our account
      任何由此所导致的费用开支由我方承担
   3. tide over the ebbing 避过退潮
   4. tallyman *n.* 船上计筹员
   5. hatchway *n.* 船舱盖

Sample 7 A Claim for Short Weight

Dear Sirs,

Re: Our Order No. 563 for 10 M/T Chemical Fertilizer

We have just received the Survey Report from Shanghai Commodity Inspection and Quarantine Bureau (SCIQB) evidencing that the captioned goods unloaded here yesterday was short weight 1,120 kg. A thorough examination showed that the short weight was due to the improper packing, for which the suppliers should be definitely responsible.

On the basis of the SCIQB's Survey Report, we hereby register a claim with you for US $ 540 in all.

We are enclosing the Survey Report No. (04) 658 and look forward to settlement at an early date.

Yours faithfully,

Notes
   1. Shanghai Commodity Inspection and Quarantine Bureau (SCIQB) 上海商品检验检疫局
   2. short weight 短重
   3. survey report 检验报告
   4. register a claim 提出索赔

Sample 8 A Settlement of the Claim

Dear Sirs,

Your Claim No. 154

With reference to your claim No. 154 for a short weight of 1,120 kg Chemical Fertilizer, we wish to express our much regret over the unfortunate incident.

After a check-up by our staff, it was found that some 28 bags had not been packed in 5-ply strong paper bags as stipulated in the contract, thus resulting in the breakage during transit, for which we tender our apologies.

In view of our long-standing business relation, we will make payment by cheque for US$ 540, the amount of claim, into your account with Bank of China, upon receipt of your agreement.

We trust that the arrangement we have made will satisfy you and look forward to receiving your further orders.

Sincerely yours,

Notes
    1. 5-ply strong paper 6ags 五层结实纸袋
    2. tender one's apologizes 表示歉意

Sample 9 A Claim on Wrong Goods

Dear Sirs,

Re: Our Order No. 367

We duly received the documents and took delivery of the goods on arrival of S.S. "Yuyuan" at Hamburg.

We thank you for your prompt execution of this order. Everything appears to be correct and in good condition except in Case No.16.

Unfortunately, when we opened this case we found it contained completely different articles, and we can only presume that a mistake was made and the contents of this case were for another order.

As we need the articles we ordered to complete deliveries to our own customers, we must ask you to arrange for the dispatch of replacement at once. We attach a list of the contents of Case No.16, and shall be glad if you will check this with our order and the copy of your invoice.

In the meantime, we are holding the above-mentioned case at your disposal, and please let us know what you wish us to do with it.

Yours faithfully,

Notes
    1. arrange for the dispatch of replacement 安排发送替换货物
    2. at one's disposal 供某人差遣，供某人处理

Chapter Ten

Sample 10   The Reply to the Above Claim

Dear Sirs,

Re: Your order No. 367 per S.S. "Yuyuan"

  Thank you for your letter of Nov. 28. We were glad to know that the consignment was delivered promptly, but it was with great regret that we heard Case No.16 did not contain the goods you ordered.

  On going into the matter we find that a mistake was indeed made in the packing, through a confusion of labels, and we have arranged for the right goods to be sent to you at once by air. Relative documents will be mailed as soon as they are ready.

  We have already faxed to inform you of this. We shall be grateful if you will keep Case No. 16 until called for by the local agent of COSCO, our forwarding agents, whom we have instructed accordingly.

  Please accept our apologies for the trouble caused to you by the error.

Yours faithfully,

Notes
  1. go into the matter 调查此事
  2. a confusion of labels 标签混乱
  3. COSCO China Ocean Shipping (Group) Company
    中国远洋运输（集团）总公司

Part III   Reading Materials

1. Negotiation[①], Mediation[②] and Arbitration[③]

  In international trade, there are many ways to settle disputes in the courts, among which the most frequently used are negotiatien, mediation or arbitration. The cost of bringing or defending a lawsuit has been increasing rapidly. The fees of lawyers have increased, the trials themselves have become much more time-consuming, which involves the time of both business people and lawyers.

  Settlement of disputes through negotiation is, therefore, a better option than going to the court.

  Many attorneys are skilled negotiators, therefore, having a competent third party to speak as an intermediary is more effective than speaking for oneself. Mediation is a voluntary process that is sometimes used when negotiation seems to fail. The parties to the disputes choose a third party to assist them in settling it. The mediator often tries first to communicate the position of the parties to each other, and then usually proposes a basis or several bases for settlement. A mediation merely facilitates negotiation, no award or opinion or the merits of the disputes are given. Mediation is especially useful in situations where the parties have some continuing relationship, because it allows them to compromise and reach a solution themselves.

Arbitration is another widely used alternative to settling disputes. Arbitration differs from mediation in that the third party to whom the dispute is submitted decides the outcome. Arbitration is often provided for in sales contract, parties who have not so provided can choose to have their dispute arbitrated after it has arisen.

2. Advantages of Arbitration

Compared with other methods of dispute resolution, arbitration has the following advantages:

- Party Autonomy

In arbitration, the parties are free to appoint arbitrators of their own choice, to select the place and language of arbitration and to determine the applicable laws. The parties may also design the arbitration proceedings to meet their special needs by agreeing on the organization of hearings, submissions of proof, and presentations of arguments. If the parties fail to reach such an agreement, it is largely left to the discretion of the arbitral tribunal of the case. As a result, arbitration is much more flexible than the procedures and timetables of national courts.

- Final and Binding

Although parties to commercial contracts have a number of options to resolve their disputes, only litigation and arbitration can provide a binding and enforceable decision.

Unlike the judgments made in litigation of first instance, arbitral awards become final and binding on the parties as soon as rendered. Even though arbitral awards may either be set aside by courts in the country where the arbitral awards are made, or be denied recognition and enforcement by courts in the country where enforcement is sought, the grounds of challenge available against the arbitral awards are very limited and in international arbitrations usually could only be based on procedural matters.

- Confidentiality

Arbitration proceedings are not open to the public. Thus, business secrets and the reputation of the parties can be effectively protected.

- International Recognition and Enforcement of Arbitral Awards[④]

Pursuant to the Convention on the Recognition and Enforcement of Foreign Arbitral Awards (The New York Convention of 1958), which has been acceded to by 144 countries so far, arbitral awards may be recognized and enforced in these contracting states. There are several other international arbitration conventions and treaties that may also help the enforcement. China acceded to the New York Convention in 1987. As a result, an arbitral award rendered in China may be recognized and enforced in 144 countries including China.

3. Arbitration Agreement

For an arbitration to take place, the disputing parties must reach an agreement in writing to submit their dispute to arbitration. This agreement may be made by incorporating an arbitration clause into the commercial contract or may be concluded after a dispute arises. The CIETAC South China recommends the following model arbitration clause to both Chinese and foreign parties:

"Any dispute arising from or in connection with this contract shall be submitted to China International Economic and Trade Arbitration Commission South China Sub-Commission for arbitration which shall be conducted in accordance with the Commission's arbitration rules in effect at the time of applying for arbitration. The arbitral award is final and binding upon both parties."

The parties may also stipulate the following items in the arbitration clause:
- the place of arbitration and/or the place of hearing;
- the language of arbitration;
- the number of arbitrators (usually one or three);
- the nationality of arbitrators;
- the applicable law of the contract;
- the application of general procedure or summary procedure.

4. Arbitration Procedure (take CIETAC South China as an example)
- Application for Arbitration

When applying for arbitration, the Claimant[5] shall submit to the Secretariat of CIETAC South China an arbitration agreement, a Request for Arbitration in writing, and the facts and evidence on which its claim is based. In addition, the arbitration fees shall be paid by the Claimant in advance according to the CIETAC Arbitration Fee Schedule. The arbitral proceedings shall commence on the date on which the CIETAC South China receives a Request for Arbitration.

- Defense and Counterclaim[7]

The CIETAC South China Secretariat shall send to the Respondent[6] the Notice of Arbitration, a copy of the Claimant's Request for Arbitration along with its attachments, the Arbitration Rules, and the Panel of Arbitrators.

The Respondent shall, within 45 days (in foreign-related arbitration) or 20 days (in domestic arbitration or arbitration where the summary procedure applies) from the date of receipt of the Notice of Arbitration, produce its written defense and relevant documentary evidence to the CIETAC South China Secretariat.

- Jurisdictional Objections[8]

The CIETAC has the power to decide on the existence and validity of an arbitration agreement and its jurisdiction over an arbitration case. The CIETAC may, if necessary, delegate such power to the arbitral tribunal.

A party may challenge the CIETAC jurisdiction if it has justified reasons. A challenge to an arbitration agreement and/or to the CIETAC jurisdiction over an arbitration case shall be raised prior to the first hearing.

- Waiver of Right to Object[9]

A party shall be deemed to have waived its right to object where it knows or should have known that any provision of, or requirement under the Arbitration Rules has not been complied with and yet participates in or proceeds with the arbitration proceedings without promptly and explicitly submitting its objection in writing to such noncompliance.

- Arbitral Tribunal[10]

According to the CIETAC Arbitration Rules, the arbitral tribunal may be composed of either a sole arbitrator or three arbitrators. A case where the summary procedure applies shall be examined and heard by a sole arbitrator, while cases where the general procedure applies shall be examined and heard by three arbitrators, unless the parties agreed otherwise. The parties may also agree on how the tribunal is formed.

Generally, the parties shall appoint arbitrators from the Panel of Arbitrators provided by the CIETAC.

Where the parties have agreed to appoint arbitrators from outside of the CIETAC's Panel of Arbitrators, the arbitrators so appointed by the parties or nominated according to the agreement of the parties may act as co-arbitrator, presiding arbitrator or sole arbitrator, subject to confirmation by the Chairman of the CIETAC in accordance with the law.

Where the parties have failed to jointly appoint the sole arbitrator or the presiding arbitrator according to the CIETAC Arbitration Rules, the sole arbitrator or the presiding arbitrator shall be appointed by the Chairman of the CIETAC.

The presiding arbitrator and the other two arbitrators shall jointly form an arbitral tribunal to examine and hear the case.

- Challenge and Replacement of Arbitrators and Majority to Continue Arbitration

Any arbitrator who has interests in a case or is related in a way that might affect the impartial examination and hearing of the case shall make a disclosure of such interests to the CIETAC, and request on his own motion for a withdrawal. The parties may also make a request for the withdrawal of an arbitrator from an arbitration case.

All arbitrators shall be independent and impartial and shall not represent either party. The CIETAC has made a set of Ethical Rules of Arbitrators to regulate the arbitrators' behavior in the conduct of arbitration cases.

- Hearing

The arbitral tribunal shall hold oral hearings when examining the case. However, oral hearings may be omitted and the case shall be examined on the basis of documents only if the parties request or agree and the arbitral tribunal also deems that oral hearings are unnecessary. Unless otherwise agreed by the parties, the arbitral tribunal may adopt an inquisitorial or adversarial approach when examining the case. The arbitral tribunal may hold deliberation at any place or in any manner that it considers appropriate.

- Place of Arbitration and Place of Oral Hearing

Where the parties have agreed on the place of arbitration in writing, the Parties' agreement shall prevail. Where the parties have not agreed on the place of arbitration, the place of arbitration shall be the domicile of the CIETAC South China. The arbitral award shall be deemed as being made at the place of arbitration.

Where the parties have agreed on the place of oral hearings, the case shall be heard at that agreed place except for circumstances stipulated in the Arbitration Rules. Unless the parties agree otherwise, a case accepted by the CIETAC South China shall be heard in Shenzhen, or if the arbitral tribunal considers it necessary, at other places with the approval of the Secretary-General of the CIETAC South China.

- Evidence

The Claimant and the Respondent shall assume the burden of proving the facts on which their claim, defense or counterclaim is based. The arbitral tribunal may undertake investigation and collect evidence on its own initiative where it deems necessary. If the arbitral tribunal investigates and collects evidence on its own initiative, it shall duly inform the parties to be present at the investigation where it deems necessary. Should one party or both parties fail to be present, the investigation and collection of evidence shall by no means be affected.

- Interim Measures of Protection⑪

To ensure the smooth administration of the arbitration proceedings and the enforcement of the awards, the parties may apply for interim measures of protection in relation to property and evidence. A party should apply in writing to the CIETAC South China for the preservation of property and/or the protection of evidence. The CIETAC South China⑫ shall forward the party's application to the competent people's court in the place where the domicile of the party against whom the interim measures are sought is located, or in the place where the property and/or the evidence is located. The CIETAC South China is only responsible for forwarding the application. The people's court shall decide whether or not the interim measures can be taken.

- Award

In a general procedure case, the arbitral tribunal shall render an arbitral award within 6 months (in foreign-related cases) or 4 months (in domestic cases) from the date on which the arbitral tribunal is formed. In a summary procedure case, the arbitral tribunal shall make an award within 3 months from the date on which the arbitral tribunal is formed. At the request of the arbitral tribunal and with the approval of the Secretary-General of the CIETAC, the time period of rendering an arbitral award may be extended.

The date on which the arbitral award is made is the date on which the arbitral award comes into effect.

The arbitral award is final and binding upon both parties. Neither party may bring a lawsuit before a court of law on the same dispute resolved by the previous arbitration or make a request to any other organization for revising the arbitral award.

- Financial Dispute Resolution

With respect to financial cases CIETAC has promulgated specifically a set of financial disputes arbitration rules and a fee schedule similar to the scale charged at the People's Court at first instance level. The time limit for adjudication is 45 working days after an arbitration tribunal is constituted. The CIETAC has engaged over 100 experts and distinguished personnel in the field of finance as arbitrators.

Notes

① negotiation *n.* 谈判，协商
② mediation *n.* 调解，调停
③ arbitration *n.* 仲裁

④ International Recognition and Enforcement of Arbitral Awards 仲裁结果在国际上的认可和执行
⑤ Claimant n. 原告
⑥ Respondent n. 被告
⑦ Counterclaim n. 反诉
⑧ Jurisdictional Objections 司法异议
⑨ Waiver of Right to Object 放弃提出异议的权利
⑩ Arbitral Tribunal 仲裁法庭
⑪ Interim Measures of Protection 临时保全措施
⑫ The CIETAC South China 中国国际经济贸易仲裁委员会华南分会

Questions

1. What are the differences among negotiation, mediation, and arbitration?
2. What are the advantages of arbitration?
3. How do you think about the process of arbitration?

Exercise

I. Fill in the blanks with the best choice:

1. We have lodged a claim _____ HBC Co. Ltd. _____ the quality of the goods shipped _____ S.S. "Nanhai."
   a. against, for, per   b. on, with, by
   c. against, under, on   d. with, for, through

2. On arrival of S.S. "Qinghai" at Port Huangpu, we _____ delivery of the consignment. Everything appears to be in good condition except in Case No. 56.
   a. took   b. made
   c. arranged   d. managed

3. They claimed compensation _____ the value _____ the missing package.
   a. of, for   b. of, of
   c. for, of   d. for, for

4. _____ the DCIB's Survey Report, we hereby register our claim with you as follows:
   a. In view of   b. On the strength of
   c. In accordance with   d. In reference to

5. We suggest that this material be packed _____ tins of 500g, 24 tins _____ one wooden case.
   a. with, in   b. in, in
   c. in, into   d. with, with

6. We regret we cannot _____ your claim.
   a. raise   b. lodge

c. entertain d. extend.

7. We are prepared to make you a reasonable _____, but not for the amount you claimed.
   a. compensation b. accommodation
   c. stipulation d. negotiation

8. This is the maximum _____ we can afford. Should you not agree to accept our proposal, we would like to settle by arbitration.
   a. concession b. commission
   c. condition d. consideration

9. We may _____ but the compensation shall, in no case, exceed US$2,000.
   a. claim b. complain
   c. compromise d. compensate

10. It would be unfair if the loss be totally _____ on us as the liability rests with both parties.
    a. taken b. imposed
    c. relied d. claimed

II. Translate the following sentences into English:
1. 如果发生索赔，必须于货到目的地后30天内提出，否则不予考虑。
2. 如果争执双方通过谈判未能达成协议，则可提交仲裁。
3. 我们可以让步，但赔偿金额无论如何不能超过800美元，否则将提交仲裁解决。
4. 检验报告证明箱子及货物受损系运输途中粗鲁搬运所致，而不是你们所说的因包装不善引起。
5. 经检查未发现任何质量低劣或工艺不佳的迹象，所用材料是上等的。
6. 我们认为供应商应对短重负责，因为青岛商检局检验证明短重1,000千克。
7. 非常抱歉我们不能考虑你方的索赔。
8. 由于双方都有责任，若全部损失都推给我方是不公平的。我们准备支付损失的50%。
9. 非常遗憾地通知你方，发给我方货物的品质与样品不符。
10. 经调查我们发现短重是由于包装时货号混淆所致。我们已安排将正确货物立即发给你方。

III. Translate the following sentences into Chinese:
1. The whole parcel is quite useless to us and we hold the goods at your disposal pending your reply. Meanwhile, we are storing them at your expense.
2. We have looked up the matter in our records, and so far as we can find, they left us in first-class condition, as our receipt from the shipping agents shows.
3. Upon examination, we find the whole of the contents stained. A great deal of them is damaged by wetting from sea water.
4. Our customers insist that they be justified in filing this claim against you for damage.
5. As we are in urgent need of the articles, we ask you to arrange for the dispatch of the replacements at once.
6. Although our contract stipulates that the goods should be packed in seaworthy packing, we can meet your special requirements for packing but the extra

expenses should be borne by you.
7. Your shipment of our Order No. 123 has been found short-weight by 500 kilos, for which we must file a claim amounting to USD 1,100 plus inspection fee.
8. The delay on your part now places us in a very serious and awkward position to our customers, and we must ask you kindly to do your best to help us out of it.
9. The wrong goods may be returned pre next available steamer for our account, but it is preferable if you can sell them out at our price in your market.
10. There is a discrepancy between the packing list of Case No. 20 and your invoice: 3 dozens Tea Service are correctly entered on the invoice but there are only 2 dozens in the case.

IV. Letter writing:

检验报告证明100件棉制品的品质比先前寄来样品差很多。写信要求退还该批货物的发票金额和检验费用共计……(make your own assumptions as to other conditions)

Chapter Eleven

Résumé, Memorandum, Notes and Fax

Part I Résumé

1. Use of a Résumé

The résumé (Am. E.), also known as curriculum vitae (Brt. E), is a document that gives a brief account of a person's basic personal facts, education, and professional background. It is often a list of separate headings, concentrating strictly on facts. A person may have different purposes at different stages of life, and different versions of a résumé are created to suit these different purposes. In one word, résumé is an outline of the highlights of your business and academic purposes; it serves as a written inventory of your strengths and qualifications.

2. Content of a Résumé

The commonly used parts:

(1) Position Objective
- Help the employer determine the position in the company suitable for you.
- May indicate your career direction, but should be brief and specific.

(2) Education
- College(s) attended, dates attended, dates of degrees.
- Major and minor, academic honors, relevant/specific courses.

(3) Employment (Experience)
- For all full-time jobs, give job title, dates, name of a company, and description of duties;
- If with a company for a number of years, highlight accomplishments;
- List part-time and temporary jobs, training and certificates if little job experience.
- Do not mention salary.

(4) Professional Activities
- Papers, presentations, publications.
- Organizations (as member, officer, etc.), committees, conferences or seminars.

(5) References
- "Upon request only." Be sure to ask permission first.
- Make certain your referees (usually three) know you professionally and can vouch for your competence.

3. Types of Résumé

There are several basic types of résumé for job hunting or other purposes depending on your personal circumstances. They are résumés in chronological format, in a functional format and in a combination of the two formats. They can also be divided into American style, British style, Chinese style, etc.

(1) Résumé in Chronological Format

This format is a list of all jobs in reverse order beginning with the most recent. It is the most common and is the easiest to read by the reader. It shows your continuous and upward career growth.

Sample 1

Jane Smith
737 Springfield Street • Vancouver, B.C. V6R 2R7
604.555.5555 • jane_smith@email.com

Summary
Software Development professional with five years experience programming in C#.Net and Java. Highly skilled in specifications gathering, troubleshooting, and quality assurance testing. Fluent in English and German.

Professional Experience
Senior Software Developer 2006—present
Initech Corporation, Vancouver, B.C.
- Developed high-transaction financial software using over five years experience in C#.NET, web services, SQL Server, AJAX, and object oriented methods.
- Coded a web-based shopping cart supporting 85,200 customers using C#.NET.
- Wrote database layer using stored procedures in SQL Server 2008.

Programmer 2004—2006
Microsoft Inc., Mission, B.C.
- Designed a three-tier object oriented architecture using web services.
- Programmed web-based financial applications in Java, C++, and C#.Net.
- Tested and verified daily software builds using quality assurance plan.

Junior Programmer 2002—2004
Education Website Builder Inc., Kelowna, B.C.
- Performed QA testing on e-Learning educational software coded in Java.
- Worked in a team with software developers and teachers to design software specifications and web interfaces for courseware database system in SQL Server.
- Tracked software bugs using Bugzilla quality assurance software.

Technical Skills
Programming Languages C#.NET, C++, Java, PHP, Python
Web Programming HTML/CSS, ASP.NET, JavaScript, JQuery
Tools MS Visual Studio, Eclipse, Subversion, Perforce
Databases SQL Server and ADO.NET, MySQL
Education B.Sc., Computer Science (High Honors), University of British Columbia, 2002

Notes
1. skilled in specifications gathering, troubleshooting, and quality assurance testing 擅长收集信息，解决问题，检测性能
2. high-transaction financial software 高额交易财务软件
3. SQL（Structured Query Language）结构化查询语言
4. a three-tier object oriented architecture 三层面向对象的体系结构
5. QA testing（Quality Assurance testing）质量保证测试

(2) Résumé in Functional Format

This format emphasizes experience, skills and accomplishments. Major functions or skills are listed with specific accomplishments below each topic. It provides a general picture of your work experience.

Sample 2

Cindy Smyth
10 Waterline Road • Toronto, Ontario, L5L 2X6
416.555.5555 • cindy_smyth@email.com

OBJECTIVE
An administrative assistant position requiring strong organization and planning skills to provide exceptional support to a vice president in the financial industry.

SKILLS SUMMARY
• Six-year experience as an office assistant supporting two senior managers in Finance and Marketing.
• Exceptional computer knowledge for analyzing reports in Excel and for building PowerPoint presentations.
• Experience with coordinating meetings within various financial departments.

SKILLS AND EXPERIENCE
ORGANIZATION AND PLANNING
• Planned and scheduled company-wide meetings for teams of senior managers.
• Coordinated time-sensitive seminars, presentations, and flights in a professional manner.
• Organized thousands of records and managed filing system containing confidential information.

COMMUNICATION
• Managed email, phone, and mail communications for senior Marketing and Finance managers.
• Responded to internal and external inquiries in a timely manner.
• Greeted visitors and directed them to appropriate offices.

COMPUTER SKILLS
• **Office Tools**   Microsoft Word, Excel, PowerPoint, and Windows Vista.
• **Internet Tools** Email, Search Engines, Website Builder.

EDUCATION AND TRAINING
George Brown College, 1996—1998, Liberal Arts
Continuing Education classes in: Microsoft Office, Accounting 1, Internet Fundamentals.

Notes
1. financial industry 金融业
2. Finance and Marketing 金融与市场营销

(3) Résumés for Job Hunting

This kind of résumé is frequently used. There are two cases: the first one is hunting for the first job after graduation. The format for it generally includes the following contents ① name, address, telephone number; ② education record: major courses and grades, optional courses; degrees and honors; ③ experiences: leading positions held at school or important activities attended; ④personal hobbies and English level; ⑤references.

The second one is for changing the job after having some working, experiences. The format in this case involves the following contents: ① name, address, telephone number; ② position apply for; ③ reasons for changing the job (complaint about the fore-employer should be avoided); ④ working experiences; ⑤ education and degrees achieved; ⑥references.

Sample 3
Résumé for Hunting for the First Job

Name Susan Jones
Address Heslington, York, YO10 5DD, UK
Telephone 44 (0) 1904 320 000
Nationality Great Britain
Date of Birth March 5, 1985

Profile
A highly responsible, well-learned and especially patient teacher with rich experiences

Education
2006—2011 University of York: Ph. D in Applied Linguistics
1999—2003 Aberystwyth University: Bachelor of Arts in English (2.1)

Employment
2007—2011 Teaching Assistant, Department of Applied Linguistics, Leeds
2003—2006 English teacher, Queenswood School

Skills
Familiar with all modern teaching facilities, a good command of English teaching methodoloy

Interests
Football, dance, and film

References available upon request

Notes
1. Bachelor of Arts in English (2.1) 英语专业的文学学士学位
2. 2.1指英国大学的学习成绩绩点，相当于美国的GPA (Grade Point Average) 3.0
3. teaching facilities 教学设施（手段）

Sample 4
Résumé for Changing the Job

LILY LEE No. 308, Ning Xia Road, Shinan District, Qingdao, 266061 Email lilylee@gmail.com Telephone 0532-82827777 Mobile 13583299999	
Objective	To obtain a more challenging position as a English-Chinese interpreter in an international company
Experience	
2012—2013	Freelance business translator, English-Chinese /Chinese-English
2011—2012	Teaching Assistant in English Department, Qingdao University
2009—2011	Volunteer Interpreter, Qingdao International Expo Center
Education	
2009—2011	Master of Arts in Translation, Qingdao University
2005—2009	Bachelor of Arts, major: English, Jinan University
Languages	Fluent English, conversational Japanese and Korean
Personal	Interests include playing basketball, reading books, travelling
References	Professor David Dong, director of translation studies center, Qingdao University,

Notes
1. Freelance Business Translator 自由商务翻译
2. Volunteer Interpreter 口译志愿者
3. Qingdao International Expo Center 青岛国际会展中心

Part II Memorandum

1. Function of a Memorandum

Memorandum, also called memo, is a short note written as a reminder. It may also be a document or other communication that helps the memory by recording events or observations on a topic:

A memorandum can be used for issuing orders, making request, informing decisions, conveying information, providing suggestions, response and instructions as reference in future, solving problems, or informal report.

2. Structure of a Memorandum

A memorandum should be organized and have a beginning, a middle and an end. It should also be proper in tone and correct in form, and its message should be clear and

concise. It usually has two parts: head and main body. The head consists of:
To: Name, Title
From: Name, Title
Subject: Treat like a Title
Date: Write out (no abbreviation)

The main body is usually made up of:
(1) Introduction: State the purpose and summarize the most important point. To be effective, the memo should deal with one issue at a time.
(2) Body: Include logically arranged details, such as facts, arguments, questions, historical background, charts, enumerated items.
(3) Conclusion: Leave the reader with some ideas of a follow-up. Consist of an IF statement that will give the reader some ideas of the next step in the process.

Sample

To: Mr. Allen Arden, Manager
From: Mr. Gary Nichols, Senior Sales Accountant
Date: April 15, 2012
Subject: Complaint from a client in Singapore

I have checked my records and I have found that Mr. Fong is correct in his complaint. I am afraid I was responsible for confusing his invoice with another invoice to Singapore. I must apologize for making this mistake.

I suggest that I write immediately to him to apologize and tell him to ignore the invoice he has. I shall then make sure that he gets a replacement invoice in the very near future.

I hope this suggestion is satisfactory.

Part III Notes

1. Use of a Note

A note is like a common letter. It is brief with only one subject, saying, invitation, apologizing, asking for leave or help, leaving messages and telephone note. The format of a note is generally very casual with the content of date, address, body, signature, etc.

Example:

2:30 p. m., Monday

Dear Dr. Hopkins,

When you read this note, please come to room No. 231, Dormitory Building No. 14. Miss Susan Hurly's father is seriously ill, and you are requested to give him an immediate treatment. Thanks .

Cordially yours,
Frank

2. Guidelines for Writing Notes

- It's unnecessary to write the year and month as the note usually takes place within the last one to two days, write down the day, or the morning, or the afternoon before the address. Sometimes the o'clock of the writing can be shown.
- The address can be casual, such as John, Mary, Zhou Lin, Dear Peter and etc.
- The content of the body should be brief and clear and the popular language is welcome, as the purpose of the note is to state the subject clearly.
- If the writer and reader have close personal relationship, the signature part can be very casual with only the name of the writer, sometimes just the surname or the given name. But in case of a note to the superior or boss, the address and ending need to be noticed.

Sample 1   Asking for Leave

Sept. 20, 2012
Dear Miss Jin,
I am not feeling very well in a feverish condition. The doctor came this morning and advised a rest of three more days. Please give an extension of a three-day sick leave, and the doctor's Certificate of Advice is enclosed.

Yours cordially,
John Marshall

Sample 2   Thank-You Note

April 28, 2012
Dear Mr. Wang,
Please accept this tie as a small token of my gratitude for the kind service you rendered me during my stay in Shanghai and I enjoyed myself there. Thank you once again. I hope you will like the tie.

With best wishes.
Yours friendly,
Tom

Sample 3   Receipt for Loan

July 20, 2011
To the Finance Department of the Institute:
I. 0. U. One Thousand Yuan (CNY 1,000) for the purchase of teaching materials.

Barbara White

Sample 4   To Rent or for Sale

Furnished house with two stories, 75 Green Street, Western Suburb, 1250 square feet, 5 bedrooms, 1 living room, private garage. Rent CAD 950 per month. Sale CAD 125,000.
Tel. 416-8852456 office time.

Sample 5   Requiring a Position

Well experienced book keeper, male, age 28, high school graduate, ten years' experience in Accounting, requiring position in this city. P.O. Box 5682.

Sample 6   A Bag Lost

In the lobby, May 25, a black square-bag with my I.D. card was missing. Finder please tells the owner. Thanks.
Tel: 65289500

Sample 7   Leaving a Message

Dear Mr. James,
Mr. Zhao Yang of "Youth Daily" has just rung up saying that he will call on you at 5:30 p. m. today.
Lilin 9: 00 a.m.

Notes

1. Please give an extension of a three-day sick leave.
   请予以续三天病假。
2. the doctor's Certificate of Advice is enclosed 随便条附上医生开具的病假证明
3. as a small token of my gratitude 略表谢意
4. I. O. U.=I owe you 我欠你

Part IV   Fax

1. Use of a Fax

Fax, the shortened form of facsimile, also called telecopying, is the transmission of printed materials, both text and images. A fax transmitter scans a document and produces electrical signals that are sent to a transmitter receiver, which makes a copy of the document. Facsimile equipment is used when a copy of a document has to be transmitted rapidly from one place to another.

2. Advantages of a Fax

- The fax can be used to communicate as fast as the international telephone call and telex. Once it is sent, the message is at the other end of the machine instantly.
- People do not have to use abbreviations as in the telegram and telex, which on

the one hand saves the trouble of memorizing them, and on the other hand avoids some unnecessary misunderstanding in their use.
- It is around-the-clock service and nobody is required to attend to the machine on the other end, so long as it is switched on.
- The fax message you send is the written record and includes sender's signature, which is very important for formal communication, especially for financial and business transactions.

3. Contents of a Fax

The fax heading usually has four basic parts.
To: Name, Title   From: Name, Title
Date: Write out, no abbreviation
Pages: Total number
Sometimes the address of the sender is printed (written) on the top of the fax.

Sample 1
Fax for Reporting Damage of the Goods

DATE	Friday, January 07, 2011
TO	Mr. Causio
FAX #	(06) 4815473
# of PAGES	1
MESSAGE	

This is an urgent request for a consignment to replace the damaged delivery which we received, and about which you have already been informed.

Please airfreight the following items:
Cat. No.   Quantity
RN30   50
AG20   70
L26   100

The damaged consignment will be returned to you on receipt of the replacement.

L. Crane
Chief Buyer

Sample 2
Fax for Inviting a Foreign Teacher

English Department
Faculty of Foreign Language
Qingdao University of Science & Technology
People's Republic of China

Feb. 9, 2012
Diana Taylor
R.4, Site 430, C.27
Courtenay, B. C. V 9N 7J3
Canada

Dear Ms. Taylor,

I'm writing in response to your January 18 fax to our university. We still have one vacancy for the status of a foreign teacher. If you are still available and interested, please let me know and send me the documents required.
Documents we need for government approval:
  1. Copies of the diploma of your highest academic degree;
  2. Detailed résumé and two letters of recommendation;
  3. Health examination record and certificate, and eight photos.

You are welcome to contact me if you have further questions. If I don't receive your reply in writing by May 25, I presume that you are not coming.

Thank you for your interest in our university.

Sincerely yours,
Li Jun
Dean
English Department

Notes
  1. letter of recommendation 推荐信
  2. You are welcome to contact me if you have further questions.
     若有疑问,欢迎和本人联系。

Appendix

Part I Abbreviations

The following are some generally accepted abbreviations and business terms.

1. Ways to abbreviate longer words:
1) to leave out vowels, e. g.

ABT	about	IMM	immediate, immediately
BFR	before		
PLS	please	INV	invoice
TKS	thanks	BF	before
YR	your	RPY	reply
CTN	carton	PCT	per cent
CNT	can not	PCS	piece

2) to retain the first syllable, e. g.

ART	article	EXP	export
AIR	airmail	IMP	import
CERT	certificate		

3) to retain the first and the last letter of a word, e. g

BK	bank	FM	from

4) to retain the important consonants and last letter of a word, e.g.

ARVD	arived		
QLy	quality	QTY	quantity

5) Some universally accepted methods to simplify the telegraphic words are regarded as regulations:

-ed (verbs)	-D	SHIPD	(shipped)
-ing (verbs)	-G	OFFERG	(offering)
-ment	-MT	PAYMT	(payment)
-tion	-TN	INSTRUCTN	(instruction)
-able	-BL	WORKBL	(workable)
-ible	-BL	POSSBL	(possible)

2. Common abbreviations in business letters:

ETA	estimated time of arrival
ETD	estimated time of departure
ETS	estimated time of sailing
FAQ	fair average quality
EMP	European Main Ports
L/C	letter of credit
B/L	bill of lading
S/C	Sale's Confirmation, Sales Contract

D/P	documents against payment
D/A	documents against acceptance
COD	cash on delivery
CAD	cash against documents
LT (R)	litre
KG	kilogram
LB	pound
OZ	ounce
MT	metric ton
DZ	dozen
S/S	steamship
MV	motor vessel
USD	U. S. Dollar
STG	pound sterling
DM	Deutsche Mark
SF (R)	Swiss Franc
EXW	Ex Works
FCA	Free Carrier
FAS	Free Alongside Ship
FOB	Free On Board
CFR	Cost and Freight
CIF	Cost. Insurance and Freight
CPT	Carriage, Paid to
CIP	Carriage and Insurance Paid to
LAF	Delivered At Frontier
DES	Delivered Ex Ship
DEQ	Delivered Ex Quay
DDU	Delivered Duty Unpaid
DDP	Delivered Duty Paid
IMP	import
EXP	export

3. Other most commonly used abbreviated expressions:

YL	your letter (we have received...)
YC	your cable (we have received...)
YT	your telex (we have received...)
ROL	referring to our letter of ...原文中没有的
ROC	referring to our cable of ...
ROT	referring to our telex of...

Part II Frequently Used Currencies

货币符号	英文货币名称	中文货币名称
AFN	Afghani	阿富汗尼

ARS	Argentine peso	阿根廷比索
AUD	Australian dollar	澳大利亚元
BRL	Brazilian real	巴西雷亚尔
BYR	Belarusian ruble	白俄罗斯卢布
CAD	Canadian dollar	加拿大元
CHF	Swiss franc	瑞士法郎
RMB	Renminbi yuan	中国人民币元
CUP	Cuban peso	古巴比索
DKK	Danish krona	丹麦克朗
EGP	Egyptian pound	埃及镑
EUR	Euro	欧元
GBP	Great British pound	英镑
HKD	Hong Kong dollar	港元
IDR	Indonesian rupiah	印度尼西亚盾
IRR	Iranian rials	伊朗里尔斯
ILP	Israeli pound	以色列镑
JPY	Japanese yen	日元
LAK	Laotian kip	老挝基普
BUK	Burmese kyat	缅甸元
MOP	Macao pataca	澳门元
MYR	Malaysian dollar	马来西亚令吉
NOK	Norwegian krone	挪威克朗
PHP	Philippine peso	菲律宾比索
RUB	Russian rouble	俄罗斯卢布
SGD	Singapore dollar	新加坡元
SOS	Somali shilling	索马里先令
TWD	New Taiwan dollar	新台币
USD	United States dollar	美元
VND	Vietnamese đong	越南盾

注：本货币符号选自ISO 4217，于国际化标准组织2008年通过，广泛用于代表货币和资金。

Part III Useful Terms

外贸函电课程专业术语是外贸函电课程的重要组成部分，在实际应用中，有时要求英译汉，有时要求汉译英。该课程专业术语多数是全称形式，但有时是缩写，形式多样。学生熟悉和掌握外贸业务中常用的词汇和术语，对今后工作有很大帮助。为了便于学习外贸函电课程的学生和有志于外贸工作的人士对这些术语的掌握和记忆，特将外贸函电专业术语按字母顺序排列，便于查阅。

A

a 2% commission (commission of 2%)　2%佣金
a complete/full set of documents　全套单据
a copy of　一份／本／册
a discount of 2%(a 2% discount)　2%折扣
a full range of samples　全套样品
a parcel of　一批
A. V. (Ad. Val)　从价运费
abide by　遵守
Acceptance Credit　承兑信用证
account for　解释
acknowledge an order　确认订单
acquaint sb. with sth.　使某人熟悉
Actual Total Loss　实际全损
additional cost　额外费用
adhere to one's commitments　忠实履行某人的义务
Advising Bank，Notifying Bank　通知银行
Agreement　协议
Air Transport　航空运输
Air Waybill　航空运单
All Risks　一切险
allow/give sb. a discount　给某人折扣
allowance　折让；允差
amend L/C　修改信用证
anticipatory L/C　预支信用证
anti-dated B/L　倒签提单
approach sb.　与……联系
approve of　赞成
Arbitral Award　仲裁裁决
Arbitration　仲裁
Arbitration Clause　仲裁条款
arrange/cover insurance　投保
arrange with sb. about / for　与某人商定
a special accommodation　作为特殊照顾
as agreed　按商定
as an exceptional case　破例
as to　就……而论，关于
Asian Development Bank　亚洲开发银行
assure sb. of sth.　向某人保证某事
at intervals of　每隔……时间
at intervals　每隔一会儿
at one's disposal　由某人处理、支配
at one's request　按某人要求
as requested　按要求

at sight　即期，一见
at your end　在你处
at your request　应你方要求
at... premium　按……保险费率
at ... rate　按……率
auction　拍卖
auctioneer　拍卖人
avail oneself of　利用

B

Back to Back Credit　背对背信用证
Balance Sheet　资产负债表
Banker's Draft　银行汇票
Banker's Reference　银行证明人
Barter　易货
be acceptable to sb.　可以为某人所接受
be acquainted with　熟悉、了解
be assured of　请放心
be available for supply　可供货
be heavily booked　订货太多
be in the market for　欲购
be of high quality　高质量的
be on the high/low side　价偏高／低
be popular　畅销
be ready for shipment　备妥待运
be strictly confidential　严守机密
be valid until　有效期至……
be within the scope of　属于……业务范围
bearer B/L　不记名提单
beneficiary　受益人
bid a price　递价
bidder　买者
bilateral trade　双边贸易
Bill of Exchange (Draft)　汇票
Bill of Lading　提单
blank endorsed　空白背书
Bona Fide Holder　合法，(正当)持有(票)人
Bonded Warehouse　保税仓库
book freight space/book shipping space　订舱
book up　订完
book/place an order with sb.　向某人订货
Breach of Contract　违约
bridge over the gap　弥补差距
Brief Credit Report　资信（情况）简报

bring down your price to...　价格降至……
bring up a claim against　向……提出索赔
broaden the market　扩大市场
business entity　企业实体
by joint efforts　通过共同努力
by separate post/mail/under separate cover　另寄，另封
by weight　按重量（计）

C

C. T. D.（Combined Transport Documents）　多式联运单据
cancel orders　撤消订单
captioned goods　标题货物
cargo receipt　承运货物收据
carry out orders　执行订单
cash account　现金账
cash against delivery　货到付款
cash against documents　凭单付款
cash payment　现金付款
cash with order　订单付款
CCPIT（China Council for the Promotion of International Trade）　中国对外贸易促进委员会
Certificate of Health (Inspection)　卫生检验证书
Certificate of Origin (Inspection)　产地检验证书
Certificate of Quality (Inspection)　品质检验证书
Certificate of Quantity (Inspection)　数量检验证书
Certificate of Value (Inspection)　价值检验证书
Certificate of Weight (Inspection)　重量检验证书
Certified Invoice　证实发票
CFR (Cost and Freight)　成本加运费
Charter Party　租船合同
Charter Party B/L　租船提单
charter ship　租船
check (cheque)　支票
check up　检查
clear off　清偿
CIF (Cost, Insurance and Freight)　成本加保险费、运费
CIP (Carriage Insurance Paid to)　运费、保险费付至
claims, arbitration　索赔、仲裁
classified catalogue　分类目录
clean B/L　清洁提单
clean bill　光票
clean credit　光票信用证

close over the gap　弥补差距
coincide with　与……一致
collecting bank　收银行
correction　托收
combined transport B/L　多式联运提单
come into effect/force　生效
come to/into the market　上市
come to terms/come to business, close a bargain/deal　达成交易
come up to　达到，符合
commercial draft　商业汇票
commercial invoice　商业发票
commission　佣金
Commodity Inspection Bureau　商品检验局
compensation trade　补偿贸易
complain about/of　抱怨
conditioned weight　公量
conditions of sale　销售条款
confirm an order　确认订单
confirm　确认书
Confirmed Letter of Credit　保兑信用证
Confirming Bank　保兑行
consignee　收货人
consignment　寄售
Consignment Note　寄售单
consignor; shipper　托运人
Constructive Total Loss　推定全损
Consular Invoice　领事发票
Container B/L　集装箱提单
Container Transport　集装箱运输
Copy B/L　副本提单
Cost and Freight (CFR)　成本加运费（……指定目的港）
Counter Offer　还盘
Counter Purchase　互购
Counter Sample　对等样品；回样
Counter Trade　对销贸易
Cover insurance　保险
CPT (Carriage Paid to)　运费付至
credit account　贷方账
Credit Limit　信贷额度
credit standing/status　信用状况
current price　现价，时价
customary practice　习惯做法，惯例

customs broker　报关行，海关经纪人
customs duties/ tariffs　关税
customs entry　进口报关
customs formalities　海关手续
Customs Invoice　海关发票

D

D/A (Documents against Acceptance)　承兑交单
D/D (Remittance by Banker's Demand Draft)　票汇
D/P (Documents against Payment)　付款交单
D/P after Sight (Documents against Payment after Sight)　远期付款交单
D/P Sight (Documents against Payment at Sight)　即期付款交单
DAF (Delivered At Frontier)　边境交货
Damage Caused by Heating and Sweating　受热受潮险
damage to the goods　货物的损害
date of delivery　交货日期
date of shipment　装运期
DDP (Delivered Duty Paid)　完税后交货
DDU (Delivered Duty Unpaid)　未完税交货
Debit Note　借记通知单；索款通知
Deferred Payment Credit　延期付款信用证
deferred payment　延期付款
delay in shipment　装运方面的延误
delay in　在……耽搁
delivery time/date　装运期
demurrage　滞期费
DEQ (Delivered Ex Quay)　目的港码头交货
DES (Delivered Ex Ship)　目的港船上交货
direct B/L　直达提单
direct steamer　直达船
dishonor　拒付
Disinfections (Inspection) Certificate　消毒检验证书
dispatch (dispatch money)　速遣费
distributor　分销
Documentary Bill　跟单汇票
Documentary Credit　跟单信用证
draw a draft on sb.　向某人开出汇票
draw samples　抽样
draw up　起草，草拟
drawee　受票人
drawer　出票人

due to arrive　预计到达

E

effect delivery　交货
effect payment　支付
EMP. (European Main Ports)　欧洲主要港口
Endorsement　背书
enjoy a good reputation　享有盛名
enjoy fast sales　畅销
enjoy popularity　受欢迎，享有盛名
enlarge/expand the market　扩大市场
enter into/establish business relations with　与……建立业务关系
equal to sample　与样品相同
establish L/C　开证
estimates time of arrival　预计到达时间
estimated time of departure　预计离港时间
EU（European Union）欧盟
ex S/S...　由……轮运来
Exclusive Agent；Sole Agent　独家代理
exclusive sales　包销
existing market　目前的市场　现存市场
expedite L/C　催证
export declaration　出口申报单
export document　出口单据
export entry　出口报关
export license　出口许可证
export quota　出口限额
export volume　出口量
extend L/C　展证
EXW (Ex Works)　工厂交货（……指定地）

F

FAQ (Fair Average Quality)　良好平均品质
FWRD (Fresh Water Rain Damage)　淡水雨淋险
fall in line with　同意，符合
fall within the business scope of　属于……业务范围
FAS（Free Alongside Ship）　装运港船边交货
FCA（Free Carrier）　货交承运人
few and far between　（船）稀少
figure in　算进，包括
file a claim against　向……提出索赔
finalize a deal/transaction　达成交易
financial standing/states　资金情况（状况）

find fault with　对……不满，挑剔
Firm Offer　实盘
firm/fixed price　固定价格
FOB (Free On Board)　装运港船上交货
FOB Liner Terms　装运港船上交货班轮条件
FOB Stowed　包括理舱费在内的装运港船上交货
FOB Trimmed　包括平舱费在内的装运港船上交货
FOB Under Tackle　装运港吊钩下交货
FOBST (FOB Stowed & Trimmed)　包括理舱费、平舱费在内的装运港船上交货
for one's account　由某人负担（费用）
for one's approval　经某人同意
for the purpose of　为……目的 / 意图
for the sake of　为了……起见 / 缘故
for your file　供你方存档
for your information/reference/consideration　供你方参考
Force Majeure　不可抗力
Foreign Exchange Reserve　外汇储备
foreign freight forwarder　国际货运
Forward Contract　远期交货合同
forwarding agent　货运代理
Forwarding Agents　运输代理人
FPA（Free from Particular Average）平安险
Franchise　免赔率
Franchise；deductible　免赔额
Free Alongside Ship (FAS)　船边交货（……指定地）
free of charge　免费
free of　免于……的，没有……的
Free on Board (FOB)　装运港船上交货（……指定装运港）
Freight　运费
Freight Prepaid　运费预付
Freight to Collect；Freight to be Paid　运费到付
from stock　供现货
frontier trade　边境贸易

G

G. A. (General Average)　共同海损
general open policy　预约总保单
Generalized System of Preference (GSP)　普惠制
goods in question　标题货物
Grade of Goods　商品的等级
Gross for Net　以毛作净
gross price　毛价
gross weight (GW)　毛重
guard against　防止，提防

H

handle claims　理赔
have heavy commitments　订货太多
have no choice but to　别无选择，只好
Heavy Weather　恶劣天气
Hedging　套期保值
honor one's draft on presentation　见票承兑
Hook Damage　钩损险

I

I. C. C. (Institute Cargo Clauses)　协会货物（保险）条款
illustrated catalogue　有插图的目录
IMF (International Monetary fund)　国际货币基金组织
Import Contract　进口合同
Import License　进口许可证
in a position to　能够
in accordance with　根据，按照，和……一致
in addition to　除……之外
in agreement with　符合，和……一致
in answer/reply to　兹复
in bad/poor condition　（表面）状况不好
in bulk　散装
in conformance/conformity with　符合，与……一致
in detail　详细地
in due time/course　及时地
in duplicate　一式二份
in good condition　（表面）状况良好
in line with the market　与市场价相符
in no case　绝不
in one's favor　以某人为受益人
in order　整齐，无误
in proportion to　与……成比例
in quadruplicate　一式四份
in regard to　关于
in reply (to one's inquiry)　答复（某人询盘）
in short/scare supply　货少
in stock　有存货
in strict confidence　严守机密
in transit　途中

in triplicate 一式三份
in two equal lots 同等数量两批
INCOTERMS (International Rules for the Interpretation of Trade Terms) 国际贸易术语解释通则
Indicative Mark 指示性标志
inferior quality 质劣
inferior to 质量次于
initial orders 首批订单
Inland Water Transportation 内河运输
Inner Packing 内包装
inquire for 询价
inquiry 询盘
inquiry sheet 询价单
insurance 保险
Insurance Broker 保险经纪人
Insurance Certificate 保险凭证；保险证书
Insurance Policy 保险单
insure... for 按……金额投保
insure... with 向……投保
insurer 承保人
insured 投保人
International Bank for settlement 国际清算银行
International Chamber of Commerce 国际商会
International Multi-modal Transport; International Combined Transport 国际多式联运
Invitation to Offer 邀请发盘
Invitation to Tender 招标
Invoice 发票
Irrevocable Letter of Credit 不可撤销信用证
ISO (International Standard Organization) 国际标准局，（国际标准化组织）
issue L/C=establish/open L/C 开立信用证

J

jerquer (customs officer attending clearance) 结关员
jerquer note （海关）结关单
joint efforts 通过共同努力
Joint Venture 合资企业

K

keep account 记账
keep sb. / advised/informed/posted of 随时通知某人……

L

L/C (Letter of Credit) 信用证
Leasing 租赁
Legal Weight 法定重量
Letter of Guarantee 保证书；保函〕
liberal quantity 充足的数量
lie within the (business) scope of 属于……业务范围
limited quantity 有限的数量
Liner B/L 班轮提单
Liner Transport 班轮运输
Liner's Freight Tariff 班轮运费表
lodge a claim 索赔
Long Form B/L 全式提单
Long Ton 长吨
Loss or Damage Caused by Breakage of Packing 包装破裂险

M

M/T (Mail Transfer) 信汇
make a counter-offer 还盘
make a mistake in 在……出错
make a reduction of... in price 减价
make allowance 折让
make an exception 破例
make an offer 报盘
make arrange for 安排
make compensation for 赔偿
make customs declaration 报关
Manufacturer's Invoice 厂商发票
maximum quantity 最大数量
measure up to 符合，达到
Measurement Ton 尺码吨
meet needs/ requirements 满足需求
meet one's obligation 履行义务、职责
meet sb. half way 各让一半
meet with （无意中）碰到
Memorandum (Memo) 备忘录
Metric Ton 公吨
minimum quantity 最小数量
moderate quantity 中等数量
more or less clause 溢短装条款
Most Favored Nation Treatment 最惠国待遇
Multilateral Trade 多边贸易
Multi-National Corporation 跨国公司

N

Negotiating Bank 议付行
Negotiation Credit 议付信用证
Net Weight 净重
Neutral Packing 中性包装
non-negotiable copy of B/L 不可转让提单副本
Non-tariff Barrier 非关税壁垒
Non-transferable L/C 不可转让信用证
Notify Party 被通知人
Nude Packed 裸装

O

ocean B/L 远洋提单
ocean marine cargo insurance 海洋运输货物保险
Ocean Transport, Marine Transport 海洋运输
on/under... terms 按……方式
on a substantial of 大规模地
on arrival of... 到达
On Board B/L, Shipped B/L 已装船提单
On Deck B/L 舱面提单
on perusal 详阅之后
on the part of/on one's part 就……而言，在……方面
on the strength of 根据，凭借
open an account 开立账户
Open Bidding 公开招标
open L/C 开证
Open Negotiation Credit 公开议付信用证
Opening Bank, Issuing Bank 开证行
Optional Port 选择港
Order B/L 指示提单
original B/L 提单正本
out of line with the market 与市场价不符
outturn sample 到货样品
overland insurance 陆运保险

P

P. A. (Particular Average) 单独海损
packing list 装箱单
packing 包装
Parcel Post Receipt 邮包收据
Parcel Post Transport 邮包运输
parent firm 母公司
partial loss 部分损失
partial shipment 分批/部分装运/船
particular average 单独海损
pass... on to for attention and reply 转交……办理答复
patent 专利
pay by installment 分期付款
pay in advance 预付
pay on delivery 货到付款
payee 收款人
payer 付款人
Paying Bank, Drawee Bank 付款行
payment by L/C 信用证支付
Payment in Advance 预付货款
Payment 付款
Penalty 罚金
per metric ton/each metric ton 每公吨
perils of the sea 海上风险
Physical Delivery 实际交货
PICC 中国人民保险公司
poor (in) quality 劣质
Port of Destination 目的港
Port of Shipment 装运港
Port Surcharge 港口附加费
Premium 保险费
present price/prevailing price 现行市价
presentation 提示
Presenting Bank 提示行
Price List 价目单
Principal 委托人
Processing Trade 加工贸易
Product Buyback 产品回购
product line 产品系列
Proforma Invoice 形式发票
Promissory Note 本票
prompt attention 立即办理
prompt shipment 即期装运
Protective Duty 保护性关税
Public Surveyor 公证行
Purchase Confirmation 购买确认书
Purchase Contract 购买合同
push the sales of 推销……
put... right 纠正
put forward 提出
put in a claim-against 向……提出索赔

Q

Quality as per Buyer's Sample 品质以买方样品为准
Quality as per Seller's Sample 品质以卖方样品为准
QUALITY, WEIGHT AND MEASUREMENTS 货物质量、重量和尺码
Quota 配额，报价

R

Rail Transport 铁路运输
Railway Bill 铁路运单
raise a claim 索赔
received for shipment B/L 备运提单
reduce your price by... 降价（多少）
refer to/referring to 参阅
refer...to... 请某人向某人了解
reference （信用、能力等的）备询人或证明人
remit... by 以……方式汇票款
remittance 汇付
Remitting Bank 汇出行
Repayment Guarantee 还款保证书
resent/revoke order 取消订单
Retail Price 零售价
Retaliatory Tariff 报复性关税
revert to... 重提；复原
Revocable Letter of Credit 可撤销信用证
Revolving Credit 循环信用证
Right of Recourse 追索权
Risk of Clash & Breakage 破损破碎险
Risk of Intermixture and Contaminations 混杂、玷污险
Risk of Leakage 渗漏险
Risk of Odor 串味险
Risk of Rust 锈损险
Risk of Shortage 短量险
Road Transportation 公路运输
rough handling 野蛮装运
ruling price 现价
Running Days 连续日
rush L/C 催证

S

S/O (Shipping Order) 装货单
Sale by Descriptions and Illustrations 凭说明书和图样买卖
Sale by Grade 凭等级买卖
Sale by Sample 凭样销售
Sale by Specification 凭规格买卖
Sale by Standard 凭标准买卖
Sales Confirmation 销售确认书
Sales Contract 销售合同
Sample Book 样本（用小块剪样装订成册，附有商品编号）
Scope of Business 业务范围
Sealed Bids; Closed Bids 密封递价
Seaworthy Packing 适合海运的包装
sell fast/well 畅销
send by separate mail/post/send separately 另寄
send herewith/ enclose 随函
Settlement of Claim 理赔
Shipping Advice 装运通知
Shipping by Chartering 租船运输
shipping instruction 装运指示
Shipping Instructions 装运（船）指示；装船（运）须知
Shipping Mark 运输标志；唛头
shipping marks 装运标记
Short Form B/L 简式提单
Short Ton 短吨
Sight Credit 即期信用证
Sight Draft 即期汇票
sight L/C 即期信用证
sign a contract 签合同
specialize in 专门经营
Stale B/L 过期提单
standard quality 标准质量
Standby Letter of Credit 备用信用证
state terms of 说明……的条款
Straight B/L 记名提单
Strikes Risk 罢工险
subject to 以……为条件
submission to tender 投标
superior quality 优质
supply from the stock 供现货
Survey Report 检验证（报告）
Symbolic Delivery 象征性交货
T. P. N. D. (Theft, Pilferage and Non-delivery)

偷窃提货不着险
T. T. (Telegraphic Transfer)　电汇
take delivery　提货
take effect/come into effect/force　生效
take out insurance　投保，办理保险
tax return　税单，纳税申报表
technical know-how　专门知识，技术诀窍
Technological Transfer　技术转让
The Metric System　公制
the quoted price　所报价格
Through B/L　联运提单
Time Charter　期租船
Time Draft (Usance Bill)　远期汇票
time of shipment/date　装运期
to one's order　凭……指定
to our mutual benefit/interest/advantage　对我们双方有利
Total Loss　全部损失，全损
Trade Barriers　贸易壁垒
trade in/deal in　经营，买卖
trade mark　商标
trade practice　贸易惯例，贸易习惯
Trade Reference　商界证明人
trade term　贸易术语，贸易条件
tramp　不定期船
Transferable Credit　可转让信用证
transit trade　转口贸易，过境贸易
Transshipment B/L　转船提单
turn down an order　拒绝订单
two items of commission　两笔佣金

U

UN (United Nations)　联合国
unclean/foul/dirty B/L　不清洁提单
Unconfirmed Letter of Credit　不保兑信用证
UNCTAD (United Nations Conference on Trade and Development)　联合国贸易和发展会议
under cover　随函附上
undertaking　保证，承担，许诺

UNDP (United Nations Development Program)　联合国国际开发署
unit price　单价
unless otherwise noticed　除非另有通知
unless otherwise provided for　除非另有规定
unloading charges　卸货费，卸车费
unloading point　卸货地点
unloading port　卸货港
usance/term/time Letter of Credit　远期信用证
usual quality　通常的质量

V

Veterinary（Inspection) Certificate　兽医检验证书
volume of exports　出口量
volume of freight traffic　货运量
volume of goods arrived　到货量
volume of imports　进口量，进口额
volume of trade　贸易额
Voluntary Offer　主动发盘
Voyage Charter　程租船

W

W/W（Warehouse to Warehouse）仓至仓条款
War Risk　战争险
warehouse receipt　仓（库）单
Warning Mark　警告性标志
Weather Working Days　晴天工作日
Weight Memo　重量单
Weight Ton　重量吨
wholesale distribution　批发商
wholesale price　批发价
With Particular Average (WPA or W. A)　水渍险
with the consent of　经……同意
withdraw an order　取消订单
within the validity of　在……有效期内
without engagement　无约束力
without recourse　无追索权
World Bank　世界银行
WTO (World Trade Organization)　世界贸易组织

参 考 文 献

1. 对外贸易经济合作部人事教育劳动司. 外经贸英语. 北京: 对外经济贸易大学出版社，2000.
2. Grahame T. Bilbow (管燕红译). 商务致胜英文书信. 北京: 外语教学与研究出版社，2004.
3. 郭继荣. 商务英语函电与沟通. 西安: 西安交通大学出版社，2008.
4. 范红. 英文商务写作教程. 北京: 清华大学出版社，2004.
5. 冯祥春，孙春立主编. 国际经贸英语文章精选(英汉对照). 北京：对外经济贸易大学出版社，2010
6. 胡英坤等. 现代商务英语写作. 大连: 东北财经大学出版社，2004.
7. 贾琰. 实用商务英语文函写作. 北京: 化学工业出版社，2004.
8. 李文彪. 国际商务函电. 北京: 北京理工大学出版社，2009.
9. 李雅静等. 涉外经贸英语函电. 青岛: 青岛海洋大学出版社，2006.
10. 孟建国. 外贸英语函电. 杭州: 浙江大学出版社，2009.
11. Philip Bedford. Import & Export. Cassell Ltd.，2002.
12. 戚云方. 新编外经贸英语函电与谈判(修订版). 杭州: 浙江大学出版社，2007.
13. 王俊主编 商务英语函电. 北京：对外经济贸易大学出版社，2011.
14. 王乃彦等. 对外经济贸易英语函电. 北京: 对外经济贸易大学出版社，2004.
15. 冼燕华主编. 国际商务英语函电. 广州：暨南大学出版社，2010.
16. 熊昌英，潘事文. 现代商务英语函电. 武汉: 华中科技大学出版社，2009.
17. 尹小莹. 外贸英语函电. 西安: 西安交通大学出版社，2004.
18. 易露霞，陈原，孙美楠. 外贸英语函电. 北京：清华大学出版社，2011.
19. 张立玉，何康民. 国际贸易进出口实务. 武汉：武汉大学出版社，2006.
20. 周瑞琪，王小鸥，徐月芳编著. 国际贸易实务（英文版）. 北京：对外经济贸易大学出版社，2011.
21. 左飚. 新编商务函电. 北京: 高等教育出版社，2008.
22. http://www.businesslink.gov.uk/
23. http://www.kingwaylogistics.com/EN/news_179.html
24. http://www.businessinsider.com/
25. http://www.24en.com/coop/ecocn/2011-03-18/132807.html
26. http://hi.baidu.com/%E8%B6%BB%A8%B6%E0%D4%DA%C9%D9%C4%EA%CD%B7/blog/item/75ea7f1fd9f3f1fc1ad5767e.html